the spice box

VEGETARIAN
INDIAN
COOKBOOK

by
Manju Shivraj Singh

Edited by Edna Z. Michael

THE CROSSING PRESS / Freedom, CA 95019

Dedicated to my husband and my four lovely daughters:
Shivina, Rupina, Shivika and Roshika

With thanks to Varsha Dandekar for editorial assistance and Paula Griffin
for typing the manuscript

Copyright © 1981 by Manju Shivraj Singh
Printed in the U.S.A.

Cover design by Mary A. Scott
Book design by Mary A. Scott and Martha J. Waters
Cover photographs by Carina Simeon

Library of Congress Cataloging in Publication Data

Singh, Manju Shivraj.
   The spice box.

   Includes index
   1. Cookery, Indic. 2. Vegetarian cookery. I. Title.
TX724.5. I4S496   641.5'636   81-3179
ISBN 0-89594-052-3   AACR2
ISBN 0-89594-053-1 (pbk.)

contents

preface

Indian cooking is not only attractive to the eye and palate—it is also good for the body in general. For instance, yogurt which recently became popular in America has always been part of an Indian meal. It is not only an effective antacid, but is also supposed to prolong life. And spices are said to stimulate the liver, a particularly useful attribute in a hot country where the liver becomes sluggish.

The Ayurvedic-Hindu science of medicine, upon which my grandmother based her medicines, recommends certain spices: ginger for rheumatism and liver complaints; cardamom for nausea, colds, fevers, hemorrhoids and eye troubles; cloves for brain and heart ailments; anise seeds for stomach disorders; chilies for paralysis; and turmeric as a fungicide and for itching and skin diseases.

I have written this book for Americans interested in vegetarian Indian cooking and for young Indians living abroad who never entered a kitchen while they were growing up. I have tried to make these recipes easy to follow. Indian food can be quite complicated in preparation, but I believe in saving time and using fewer ingredients whenever possible.

I am grateful to the Maharani Gayatri Devi School in Jaipur where I learned to cook my first curry. I am also grateful to my mother who gave me the opportunity to learn exotic curry dishes and dishes of international origin. I have always wanted to share my recipes with the world. Happy currying to all of you!

—Manju Shivraj Singh

introduction

Curries

Curries have traveled around the world and are now a household word. The explanation is simple. The tongue becomes a slave to the flavor of curry—it is an addiction. The spices used may be fresh or dried: onions, ginger root, garlic, turmeric, coriander, red chili, cumin, cloves, cinnamon and so on. The degree of heat in the curry in India varies from house to house and from city to city. The recipes in this book can be adjusted to your own taste, either hotter or milder.

Curries can be cooked in many colors: red, green, yellow and white. The red color is derived from tomato puree, green from ground spinach or fresh mint, yellow from plenty of turmeric, white from milk and yogurt. Four color curries are attractive on a table served along with any of the following: chopped roasted peanuts, chopped tomatoes, sliced cucumbers, sliced bananas, bell peppers, onions, papaya, apples, radishes, hard-boiled eggs, peeled tangerines, raisins, sliced roasted coconut, sweet mango chutney, hot mango pickles, fried popadams, roasted and diced Bombay duck, grated carrots, pickled onions, fresh sliced onions, fresh mint chutney, fresh coriander chutney, pickled cucumbers, grated fresh coconut. These items can be placed in colorful bowls around the curry platter.

Dals

Anything that is a dried legume we cal a *dal*. The word *dal* is therefore used for soups, either thick or thin. When you add a *masala* (spices) to the *dal,* you have a curry.

Dals are frequently called the poor man's meat because they are the main source of protein for the poor in India. Most Indians are happy to eat *dal* and *roti* (bread) twice a day, served along with some vegetables.

Dals may be prepared by boiling them in water in a saucepan or pressure cooker, the length of time depending on the *dal*. They may also be sprouted and served in salads. Or they may be sprouted first and then boiled. If you sprout the *dals* before you eat them, the vitamin content of the *dals* is higher. Also, if you boil the sprouted *dals,* the cooking time will be shorter.

We have many *dals*. Here are a few:

chana dal—split yellow chickpeas, used in *baghars* and chutneys.

urad dal—split black gram, white in color, used in *baghars* and in South Indian dishes which are fermented.

kabli chana—whole chickpeas, cream colored, used in curries, Punjabi style.

lobia—black eyed peas, used in curries.

masoor dal—small pink lentils which turn yellow after cooking, used in curries and soups.

matar dal—split green peas, used in curries.

moong dal—mung beans, used in rice dishes and curries

sabat masoor—green lentils, used in soups and curries.

safed moong—split mung beans, pale yellow in color, used in rice dishes and curries.

toor dal—pigeon peas which look like yellow split peas, used in curries.

Spices and Other Flavorings

Allspice *(Kabab Cheeni)*
The flavor is similar to a blend of several spices such as cloves, cinnamon and pepper. It has a bitter, hot taste and is slightly numbing to the tongue. It can be used as a substitute for *garam masala* (see page 16).

Anise Seed *(Sonf)*
Considered a cousin to cumin seed, it has a sweet, pungent taste. It is used in curries and fried snacks. The seeds are often roasted and kept in a bottle to be eaten after meals as an aid to digestion. Often small bowls of roasted anise seeds are found on tables in Indian restaurants.

Asafetida *(Heeng)*
This is a resin that you can use powdered or in lump form. A small amount is sometimes used in curries for a rich flavor. It is claimed that asafetida aids digestion.

Carom Seeds *(Ajwain)*
Sometimes called lovage, these seeds resemble celery seeds. Their piquant flavor is used for Indian main dishes.

Cardamom *(Elaichi)*
This is a seed or a dried fruit of a flowering plant belonging to the ginger family. The seeds are enclosed in fibrous green or black pods. The seeds are used in *garam masala*. In northern India the whole pods are used in cooking. Many Indians carry cardamom seeds in small pill boxes to chew. It, too, has a digestive effect.

Chilies, Green *(Hari Mirch)*
Chilies are easily grown. The best come from Kashmir, Hungary and the West Indies. Green chilies add heat and zest to curries and are also a good source of vitamin C. They are used in pickles, chutneys, curries and in yogurt salads *(raitas)*. Fresh green chilies are available

in Oriental stores; if fresh chilies are not available, canned jalapeños can be used instead.

The smaller the chilies the hotter they generally will be. If you like your food very hot, do not seed the chilies when you prepare them.

Chilies, Red *(Lal Mirch)*

Red chilies are ripe chilies that have been dried in the sun. They are usually toasted before grinding or soaked in water and then ground. Red chilies add red color to the curry. They must be treated with respect as the hot or mild flavor of the curry is determined by the amount used. It is also used as a preservative in pickles. If eaten in large quantities, red chilies may cause stomach ulcers. Careful handling of the chilies is of utmost importance because the released oils can burn your eyes and skin for several hours. It is best to avoid direct contact.

Cinnamon Stick *(Dalchini)*

These look like long brown cigars but are actually pieces of dried young bark. Cinnamon is a sweet aromatic spice and has a powerful numbing and antiseptic effect. It is usually used in broken pieces to flavor rice and lentils. It is also used in *garam masala* powder (see Index).

Coriander *(Dhania)*

Coriander has a flavor reminiscent of orange peel and honey. Dried coriander seeds are round and pale brown in color. One of the basic spices of curry powder, it is used in large amounts in curries and in pickles, chutneys and vegetables.

Green coriander leaves or Chinese parsley is a great favorite of curry lovers. They can be grown in your kitchen garden by slightly crushing the seeds with a rolling pin and soaking them overnight. Plant them in a box the next morning and water on alternate days. They will sprout within a week. They can be used in freshly ground chutneys and for garnishing curries.

Cumin *(Zeera)*

Cumin has a warm and powerful aroma. It is the ripe seed of a plant that comes from the same family as caraway, coriander and anise seed. One of the most important spices, it is used either whole or powdered to flavor curries. Cumin seeds can be roasted on an iron griddle and then ground into a fine powder. The powder is kept in a jar to season yogurt salads, cooked vegetables and curries.

Sometimes cumin seeds are fried in a little hot oil to release their flavor prior to adding the other ingredients. This technique removes the raw flavor from the spice at the same time that it flavors the oil.

Curry Leaves *(Kari Patta)*

These can be bought dried at any Indian grocery store. In India people mostly grow them in their kitchen gardens and use them fresh.

Fenugreek *(Maithi)*

Related to the lentil family, fenugreek seeds are very tiny and rock-hard, with a bitter flavor. They are used in small quantities in cooking vegetables, pickles, soups and legumes. Ground seeds help to thicken curries. They are supposed to help diabetics and to bring down fevers.

Garlic *(Lahsun)*

No curry is complete without garlic. In India we grind our garlic fresh every day but it is also available in powdered form. Garlic is considered good for the health in general and specifically for the digestion. Many Indians believe that garlic and onions help remove cholesterol thereby keeping the blood in good working order. Therefore, many Indians take garlic pills every day along with their vitamin pills.

Fresh Ginger *(Adrak)*; Dried Ginger *(Sonth)*

The ginger plant is a reedy, tropical bamboo-like plant. Ginger root develops in the ground where it sprouts a number of knobby lobes. The roots are dug up, sun-dried and then marketed whole or powdered.

Ginger, a very ancient spice, was used in medieval times as a medicine to prevent diarrhea. In India, fresh ginger is used daily, either peeled, ground into a paste or chopped in vegetables and lentils. It has a pungent, hot flavor. One teaspoon of ginger paste heated with one teaspoon of lemon juice is often taken in small amounts to soothe a sore throat. Fresh ginger is preferable to dried ginger.

Mace, Nutmeg *(Javitri, Jaiphal)*

Mace and nutmeg are the only two spices found on the same plant. Mace blades are the orange tendrils that lie around the shell of the nutmeg. Their flavors are very similar; both add a warm flavor. Mace has a milder, less bitter flavor than nutmeg. Nutmeg is soporific even in small quantities and is narcotic and emetic in large quantities. Neither is used extensively in curries.

Mango Powder *(Amchur)*

Mango powder is tart and can be used as a substitute for lemon juice. It may be purchased in Oriental stores.

Mustard Seed *(Rai)*

Mustard seeds are black, brown or yellow. They have a unique, nutty flavor when roasted. Mustard seeds are used to flavor curries, pickles and chutneys in south India whereas in the north, cumin is used instead.

Peppercorns *(Kali Mirch)*

Peppercorns, or whole black peppers, are dried fruits or berries which grow on climbing vines. They should be freshly ground to be most effective. Sometimes they are used as a whole, uncrushed condiment. In India peppercorns are exported to the western countries. Since peppercorns are a good cash crop and are hard to grow, Indians use red and green chilies instead.

Poppy Seeds *(Khus Khus)*

Poppy seeds have a nutty flavor. They are roasted on an iron griddle and then ground with or without water. They are used to thicken curries only on special occasions. Sesame seeds may be substituted.

Sesame Seeds *(Til)*

Sesame seeds are small and oval shaped. They are used in curries to add flavor or as a thickening agent. They are usually roasted in a hot pan and then ground. They are also used in pickles and chutneys. Ground roasted peanuts can be substituted for sesame seeds.

Tamarind *(Imli)*

Tamarind is the sour fruit of the tamarind tree. It adds a sour taste to vegetables, *dals,* meats and other foods. The sour, brown pulpy pod is dried in the sun and then stored. When ready to use, it is soaked in a little water and then squeezed out. The pulp and seeds are thrown out but the thick, gravy-like water is strained and used for cooking. Lemons, limes, mangoes, mango powder, or green apples are excellent substitutes. Dried black tamarind slabs can be bought in Oriental stores and stored for over a year.

Turmeric *(Haldi)*

Turmeric is used in all curries and gives them the characteristic bright yellow hue. Like ginger, to which it is closely related, it is an aromatic root and has the combined properties of a spice and a dye. It has been used as both since ancient times. Every day for seven days before the wedding ceremony, brides rub their bodies, hands, legs and faces with turmeric mixed with oil and gram flour to give the skin a fresh glow.

Saffron is often substituted for turmeric in sweet dishes and rich rice *biryanis.*

Mixtures of Spices

Garam Masala, Powdered

Garam masala is a spicy mixture which is always used, either whole or powdered, to flavor curries. In north India *garam masala* is freshly ground daily. It will remain fresh if stored in an airtight jar. Commercial *garam masala* is available—Rajah is a good brand.

1 tablespoon whole black peppercorns
16 whole cloves
6 whole cardamom seeds (green)
1 inch piece of cinnamon stick
1 teaspoon whole black, small cumin seeds
2 bay leaves
2 teaspoons whole cumin seeds

Grind all of the above ingredients in a coffee grinder or pepper mill and store in an airtight jar. It is important to have this on hand.

Garam Masala, Whole (*Garam* means hot and *masala* means spice.)

4 teaspoons whole peppercorns
4 teaspoons whole cloves
4 teaspoons whole black cumin seeds
4 teaspoons whole green cardamom seeds
4 pieces of cinnamon
4 big black cardamom seeds

Mix all the above whole spices and keep in a jar with a tight lid or in a spice box.

Curry Powder

2 teaspoons turmeric powder
4 teaspoons cumin powder
8 teaspoons cayenne pepper
16 teaspoons coriander powder

Mix and store in a jar or can with a tight lid.

Sambhar Powder

Roast each of the following items separately in a dry pan:

1 cup coriander seeds
½ cup whole red chilies
2 teaspoons whole fenugreek seeds
2 teaspoons whole cumin seeds
1 teaspoon whole black peppercorns
2 sticks of cinnamon, each about 3 inches
1 tablespoon yellow split peas
1 tablespoon washed *urad dal*
½ teaspoon asafetida
1 tablespoon dried shredded coconut

When all the above ingredients are roasted, grind into a fine powder in the electric blender or coffee grinder. Mix well and store in an airtight jar for future use. This will last a long time.

Spiced Salt *(Chaat Masala)*

We use spiced salt in salads *(chaats)*. We make it by mixing together equal quantities of roasted ground cumin seeds, black pepper, coriander and red chili. It is then stored in an airtight jar.

Though this is called spiced salt, it contains no salt at all.

Basic Procedures

Badi (dried ground mung bean drops)

2 cups mung beans
water to cover
salt to taste
2 teaspoons cayenne pepper
2 teaspoons cumin seeds
1 teaspoon turmeric powder
a pinch of asafetida
2 fresh green chilies, seeded and chopped

Soak mung beans overnight. Drain and grind (see Grinding Dals on page 19 for directions on grinding beans). Add salt, cayenne pepper, cumin seeds, turmeric, asafetida and green chilies.

Grease a cookie sheet or a large plate and drop the mung bean batter by the teaspoonful about 2 inches apart. Dry for 2-3 days in the sun. Turn them over and dry them again in the sun for 2-3 days.

(These can be dried in an oven at 100 degrees for 3 hours. The result, however, is not as satisfactory.)

The *badis* after drying should be stored in an airtight tin. They can be fried and cooked with a curry of potatoes or eggplant. They are good when fresh vegetables are not readily available.

These may be purchased in an oriental store.

Baghar

A seasoning made by heating oil in a small frying pan or saucepan, adding cumin or mustard seeds and frying these seeds till they pop, then adding garlic, red chili, etc.

Breaking Open a Coconut

Some take the primitive approach and smash the coconut on any hard surface like a sidewalk. Others take a hammer and nail and pierce the shell. Either way, drain off the juice. Place the coconut in a 350 degree oven for 30 minutes. Tap it with a hammer so that the hard shell comes off in large pieces. Using a paring knife, cut off the thin brown shell covering the white meat.

Coconut Milk

Grate the meat of a fresh coconut and boil it in 1 cup water for 20 minutes. Put through a sieve and apply some pressure. Discard pulp. Fluid is coconut milk.

Or you can blend chunks of coconut with water until smooth. Strain. The taste is better this way.

Cumin Seeds, Roasted

Heat a heavy ungreased frying pan and roast whole cumin seeds till they turn slightly darker. Stir while you fry them. Cool and grind in a blender or coffee grinder to a fine powder. Store in an airtight bottle.

Curds

Place unflavored yogurt in a muslin bag. Let it drip until no more water emerges from the bag. Squeeze the bag with your hands to ease out the remaining water. This will be of crumbly consistency, like cottage cheese.

Ghee (clarified butter)

Heat butter over low heat and let simmer until the water in the butter evaporates. Place in refrigerator for 4 hours. The clarified butter will float to the top. Spoon it out into another pan and boil for 2 minutes. Strain through a muslin cloth. Cool and store in an airtight jar.

Grinding Dals

Soak the *dals* overnight in water to cover. Drain, reserve fluid. Put in blender. Add just enough fluid so that mixture grinds easily.

Grinding Spices

Use either a mortar and pestle, a coffee or seed grinder, or a blender.

Paneer (homemade Indian cheese)

Bring 6 cups milk to a boil. Add the juice of 3 lemons or 3 cups of buttermilk. Stir until milk curdles. Cover it and set aside 20 minutes.

Strain through a damp muslin cloth and squeeze out all the fluid. Tie a knot in the muslin and put it under a heavy weight (a filled quart jar will do) for about 4 hours. Take it out and cut into small squares. It will be the consistency of a heavy tofu.

We often fry *paneer* and eat it by itself or we put it into a curry.

Poppadams

1 cup *urad dal*
salt to taste
1 teaspoon cayenne pepper
½ teaspoon crushed black peppercorns
a pinch of asafetida
¼ cup water

Soak the *urad dal* overnight. Drain and dry in the sun the next day. Grind into a powder. Mix all the ingredients together and make a stiff dough with water. Roll out the dough into thin circles. Dry them in the sun for 1-2 days until completely dry and store in an airtight tin. These can be fried crisp in hot oil before serving. A *must* for every curry dinner.

These can be purchased in Oriental stores.

Sprouts

1 cup mung beans *or*
    any *dal*
3 cups water

Soak the mung beans in water for 24 hours. Drain and tie in a wet muslin cloth overnight. Wet the muslin again in the morning. Sprouts will appear quickly in warm weather, less quickly in cold weather.

Tamarind Water *(Imli Paani)*

1 tablespoon dried tamarind
1 cup water

Soak tamarind in water for 2 hours. Squeeze through a sieve. Throw away the pulp.

Yogurt

2 cups milk
1 teaspoon yogurt or yogurt culture

Heat milk to body temperature. Add yogurt or yogurt culture and stir. Keep overnight in a warm place, covered with a tea cosy or several towels. It is ready the next morning. A ceramic or earthenware bowl gives the best results.

If you buy yogurt, buy only unflavored, unsweetened yogurt to serve with Indian dishes.

Utensils, Gadgets and Tools

Preparation of Indian food requires some equipment which goes a little beyond the repertoire of the standard kitchen.

1. You will need something to grind the spices. In India, a grinding stone used to be common in every kitchen. Nowadays it is being replaced by the blender, electric seed grinder, food processor or coffee grinder. You can use a mortar and pestle as a western equivalent of the grinding stone.

2. A wok *(karahi)* is one of the basics. The wok's round bottom helps to fry food fast in a small amount of oil. It is also used for making syrup and dipping or soaking desserts.

3. Heavy pans with lids are necessary. We call them *bhagonas* or *dekchi.*

4. A pressure cooker aids in cooking time-consuming Indian recipes.

5. You should have a rolling pin *(belan)* and board *(chakla)* to make *chappatis,* rolled bread. You can also use these to crush dry ingredients such as black pepper, cumin seeds, mustard seeds and garlic.

6. You will need a cast-iron griddle *(tawa)* for roasting *chappatis* or spices or making rice pancakes *(dosa).*

7. You will need various kinds of spoons for stirring and frying curries: a spoon which is flat on both sides, like a spatula, and one with holes in it for passing batter through into hot oil.

8. A metal grater which can grate, shred and make chips.

9. Tongs are used in Indian kitchens in place of pot holders. They are helpful in frying *poppadams* and in charcoal cooking.

10. A scale.

11. A betel nut cutter *(sarota)* to slice not only betel nuts but almonds and pistachios.

12. A sieve *(sancha)* through which you can press batters to make salty, vermicelli-like snacks *(sev).* A ricer can be used instead.

13. A spice box *(masala dibba).*

Where to Buy Indian Foods

This is only a sampling of stores that sell Indian food in the U.S.A. Try your local oriental store first; if you can't find what you want, this list may help.

WEST COAST

Bazaar of India
1331 University Avenue
Berkeley, CALIFORNIA 94702

Porter's Foods Unlimited
125 W. 11th Avenue
Eugene, OREGON 97401

Specialty Spice House
Pike Place Market
Seattle, WASHINGTON 98105

EAST COAST

India Health Foods
1169 State Street
Bridgeport, CONNECTICUT 06605

Cambridge Coffee, Tea and Spice House
1765 Massachusetts Avenue
Cambridge, MASSACHUSETTS 02138

Cardullo's Gourmet Shop
6 Brattle Street
Cambridge, MASSACHUSETTS 02138

Aphrodisia Products, Inc.
28 Carmine Street
New York, NEW YORK

Foods of India
81-16 Broadway
Queens, NEW YORK
(This is the store I used while I lived in Ithaca. I would phone in my order (212-426-6071) and they would mail my groceries to me.)

India Food Mart
808 South 47th Street
Philadelphia, PENNSYLVANIA 19143

House of India
5840 Forward Avenue
Pittsburgh, PENNSYLVANIA 15217

MIDWEST

India Gifts and Foods
1031-33 Belmont Avenue
Chicago, ILLINOIS 60650

India Groceries
5002 N. Sheridan Road
Chicago, ILLINOIS 60640

India Foods and Boutique
3729 Cass
Detroit, MICHIGAN 48201

Quality Imported Foods
717 N. Sixth Street
St. Louis, MISSOURI 63101

Indian Groceries and Spices
2527 W. National Avenue
Milwaukee, WISCONSIN 53208

International House of Foods
440 West Gorham Street
Madison, WISCONSIN 53703

SOUTHWEST

Antone's Import Company
4234 Harry Hines Blvd.
Dallas, TEXAS 75219

Antone's Import Company
8111 S. Main Street
Houston, TEXAS 77006

appetizers and snacks

These recipes can be served as snacks at any time of day or evening or as appetizers. They are particularly good served with a fresh chutney.

A Word of Explanation:

Samosas are savory, filled pastries which are deep-fried. They are never sweet.

Pakoras are fritters which are prepared by dipping pieces of vegetables or fruits or cheese in batter and then deep-frying them.

Dhoklas are made of a fermented batter which is put into molds and steamed. When cooked, these have a spongy texture.

Idlis are like dumplings. They are made of a fermented batter placed into molds and steamed. They are moister than the *dhoklas* and not as spongy.

Dosas are like porous crepes but are made of fermented batter. These are oily to the touch whereas crepes are dry.

Deep-Fried, Filled Pastries *(Samosas)*

The *samosa* is a delicious savory that is especially good for a cock-tail party. It can be made into large, medium or bite-size portions. It is triangular and satisfies everyone's angularities. Usually, the fill-ing for *samosas* is curried potatoes.

Potato Filling:

2 tablespoons oil
½ teaspoon cumin seeds
1 medium onion, thinly sliced
½ inch piece ginger root, sliced
1 teaspoon coriander powder
½ teaspoon turmeric powder
½ teaspoon cayenne pepper
1 teaspoon salt
½ teaspoon anise seed
2 medium potatoes, boiled, peeled, mashed or cubed
¼ cup green peas, cooked
juice of 1 lemon or 1 teaspoon mango powder

Pastry Shell (*samosa* covering):

2½ cups all-purpose flour
½ teaspoon salt
½ teaspoon baking powder
2 tablespoons oil or *ghee* (see page 19)
½ cup water
2 cups vegetable oil for deep-frying

For the Filling:

Heat the oil in a heavy skillet. Add the cumin and fry until the seeds are brown. Quickly add and fry the thinly sliced onion and the ginger. Add the coriander, turmeric and cayenne (they form the curry powder), salt and anise seed. Add a dash of water and brown well. Remove from heat. Add potatoes and peas, lemon juice (or mango powder). Mix together thoroughly. Set aside to cool.

For the Shell:

Sift the flour, salt and baking powder into a deep bowl. Make a well in the center and pour in the oil or *ghee*. Make a stiff dough by gradually adding the water and kneading it. Divide the prepared dough into 16 equal parts and form them into balls. Roll out each ball into a thin flat round circle, about 4 inches in diameter. Cut in half and form a cone by wetting the corner with wet fingers. Fill in the cone with the filling of curried peas and potatoes. Seal the open end of the cone with water, pressing firmly. Prepare all the *samosas* and cover them up with a damp dishcloth.

Heat oil for frying and deep-fry 4 or 5 *samosas* at a time for about 2 to 3 minutes until golden brown on both sides. Drain them on paper towels and serve hot. These can be served with ketchup or any chutney.

Yields: 32

Potato/Tapioca Balls *(Sabudana Vada)*

½ cup tapioca
3 cups water
4 medium potatoes, unpeeled
5 fresh green chilies, seeded
6 teaspoons chopped green coriander leaves
3 teaspoons chopped ginger root
1 egg
salt to taste
¼ cup semolina (Cream of Wheat)
2 cups oil for frying

Soak tapioca overnight in 3 cups of water. Strain and squeeze out remaining water. Boil potatoes until tender. Peel and grate them. Mix grated potatoes and tapioca into a smooth mixture.

Grind green chilies, green coriander and ginger to a smooth paste. Beat the egg with a whisk and incorporate into paste. Add egg to the potato mixture. Then salt to taste. Shape into small balls and roll in semolina. Deep-fry in hot oil over medium heat until golden brown. Serve hot with a chutney or any preferred sauce.

Yields: 18

Deep-Fried Fritters *(Pakoras or Bhajyas)*

This is a snack eaten throughout India by the rich and poor. Making fritters is a popular pastime during the rainy season when everyone is indoors. The recipe I give here is the basic one on which variations can be made. Any raw vegetable—sliced onions, round slices of raw potatoes, cubed eggplant, thinly sliced cauliflower, chopped spinach or chopped green chilies—can be dipped in the basic batter and fried.

> 2 cups chickpea flour
> 1 fresh green chili, seeded and sliced
> 1 large onion, chopped
> 1 teaspoon cumin seeds
> ½ teaspoon cayenne pepper
> salt to taste
> 2 teaspoons *garam masala*, powdered (see page 16)
> a few mint or green coriander leaves, chopped
> ½ teaspoon baking powder
> ½ to ¾ cup cold water
> 2 cups oil for frying

In a deep bowl, combine all the ingredients except the water and oil for frying. Start mixing with a fork or your hand; add water slowly until you have a thick paste.

Heat 2 cups of oil in a wok or a deep pan. Drop the batter by the tablespoon in the oil bit by bit, forming them into fritters. When they are lightly browned, turn them over with a frying spoon and let them cook properly. Do not overcook. Drain the fritters on a paper towel.

Serve hot with a chutney.

Yields: 30

Egg Fritters *(Pakoras)*

1 dozen eggs, hard-cooked, peeled and halved

Fritter Batter, Traditional:

> 1 cup chickpea flour
> ¼ teaspoon turmeric powder
> ¼ teaspoon salt
> dash cayenne pepper
> 1 teaspoon cumin seeds
> ¼ teaspoon baking soda
> ½ cup water (approximately)
> 2 cups oil for frying

Fritter Batter, Americanized

> 1½ cups all-purpose flour
> ¼ teaspoon salt
> dash of cayenne pepper
> ½ teaspoon baking powder
> ½ cup milk
> 1 egg
> 2 cups oil for frying

Mix either batter with your hand or a wooden spoon. Add liquid slowly to get the consistency of a pancake batter. Dip the egg halves in batter and deep-fry, one at a time.

Yields: 24

Variations: Instead of eggs, use ¼ lb. Indian cheese (page 20) cut in 1 inch cubes, or pieces of raw vegetables. Or you may incorporate ¼ cup roasted peanuts and ¾ cup cooked, drained, chopped spinach into the batter.

Fried Bean Fritters *(Vadas or Vadai)*

1 cup *urad dal*
2 fresh green chilies, seeded
1 inch piece of ginger root
6 curry leaves (optional)
a few chopped coriander leaves
salt to taste
juice of 1 lemon
2 cups oil for frying

Soak the *urad dal* for 2 hours. Wash the skins off and drain. Grind them into a paste, using a blender (see page 19 for directions).

Chop the chilies, ginger, curry leaves and coriander leaves.

Mix all ingredients except the oil for frying and form into small balls. On a piece of wax paper flatten the balls and make a hole in the centers with your finger.

Slowly drop these into deep oil and fry till evenly browned.

Serves: 8

Bread Fritters (Pakoras)

½ cup of any chutney
12 slices of bread, rye or white
fritter batter (see page 30)
2 cups oil for frying

Spread the chutney on six slices of bread and cover with the other six slices to make sandwiches. Cut into large triangles. Dip the triangles into the fritter batter and deep-fry, one at a time.

Serves: 12

Stuffed Bread Fritters (Pakoras)

4 medium potatoes, boiled, peeled and mashed
1 teaspoon curry powder
salt to taste
juice of 1 lemon
½ teaspoon cumin seeds
1 fresh green chili, seeded and chopped
1 medium onion, chopped
12 slices of bread, rye or white
fritter batter (see page 30)
2 cups oil for frying

Combine all the ingredients except the bread, batter and oil. Soak the bread, one slice at a time, in water, remove quickly and squeeze out the water. Place the soaked bread on your left hand. Place a spoonful of mashed potato filling in the center of the bread and fold it firmly width-wise. Dip the prepared bread into the batter and fry one at a time. Serve with tomato ketchup.

Yields: 12

Stuffed Green Chili Fritters
(Hari Mirch Pakoras)

12 large fresh green chili peppers
2 teaspoons brown sugar or molasses
salt to taste
4 medium potatoes, boiled, peeled and mashed
a few mint leaves, chopped
1 teaspoon mango powder or juice of lemon
fritter batter (see page 30)
2 cups oil for frying

Remove seeds from green chili peppers by slitting them on the side. Mix the sugar, salt, potatoes, mint and mango powder. Fill the green chilies through the slits. Dip the chilies one by one into the fritter batter and deep fry them two at a time. Drain and serve hot with ketchup.

Serves· 12

Note: If you use hot chili peppers, the result will be hot. If you prefer something milder, use the large, light green, long peppers. You may have to double the filling.

Potato Fritters (Aloo Bonda)

This is the second most popular Indian dish, after *samosas*. It may be found in Indian restaurants around the world.

4 medium potatoes, boiled, peeled and mashed
1 teaspoon cumin seeds
1 medium onion, finely chopped
1 fresh green chili, seeded and finely chopped
juice of 1 lemon
a few mint or coriander leaves, chopped
salt to taste
½ teaspoon cayenne pepper
fritter batter (see page 30)
2 cups oil for frying

Combine all the ingredients except the fritter batter and the oil for frying. Mix well. Make into balls the size of a lemon. Dip each ball into the fritter batter and deep-fry in a wok. Serve hot with a mint chutney or ketchup.

Serves: 12

Yogurt and Fritter Salad *(Dahi Baras)*

The Balls:

1 cup *urad dal* (see page 10)
1 fresh green chili, seeded
salt to taste
Pinch of asafetida
2 cups oil for frying
salt water (½ teaspoon salt to 2 cups water)

Yogurt Mixture:

4 cups yogurt
salt to taste
1 teaspoon cayenne pepper
1 teaspoon *garam masala* powder (see page 16)
3 teaspoons cumin seeds, roasted and powdered
coriander leaves for garnishing

Soak *urad dal* in water overnight. Drain and grind in blender to form a paste. While grinding add 1 green chili, salt and a pinch of asafetida. Heat the oil in a wok or *karahi*. Fry small balls of the paste in the hot oil. When the fritters are brown, remove and put them in salted water for 5 minutes. Remove and squeeze out the water. Meanwhile, tie the 4 cups of yogurt in a muslin cloth and let the water drip out for an hour or two. Remove. Add a little salt, cayenne pepper and *garam masala* powder to the yogurt. Spoon the yogurt over the balls of *urad dal*. Sprinkle the roasted cumin powder on top of the yogurt along with chopped fresh or dried coriander leaves.

Serves: 8

Note: the soaking in salt water removes the oil from the fritters and makes them softer.

For instructions on grinding the *urad dal*, see page 19.

Potato Patties *(Aloo Ki Tikki)*

Filling:

1 medium onion, chopped
1 tablespoon oil
1 teaspoon cumin seeds
½ cup green peas, cooked
salt to taste
1 fresh green chili, seeded and chopped
½ teaspoon turmeric powder
1 teaspoon coriander powder
2 pinches chopped coriander leaves

Outside of Patty:

2 cups mashed potatoes
salt to taste
1 teaspoon *garam masala* powder (see page 16)
1 teaspoon cayenne pepper
juice of 1 lemon

For the Filling:

Fry the onion in oil with cumin seed until lightly browned. Add cooked green peas, salt to taste, green chili, turmeric, coriander and a few chopped coriander leaves. Fry for a few minutes. Put aside.

For the Patty:

To the mashed potatoes add salt, *garam masala* powder, cayenne pepper and lemon juice. Mix and knead thoroughly with your hand. Divide the potatoes into 12 equal balls. Flatten each ball in the greased palm of your hand and put one tablespoon of filling on the flattened ball. Close the potato ball and flatten it evenly. Using all of the potato mixture, make 12 patties. Heat a cast-iron frying pan or a *tawa* and grease it with oil. Put patties in the pan, four at a time, and fry over medium heat until nicely browned. Turn over with a flat spatula and fry on the other side. Pour some oil around the patties so they do not burn.

Yields: 12

Chickpeas or Garbanzos *(Chola)*

2 tablespoons cooking oil
½ teaspoon cumin seeds
2 medium onions, grated
6 cloves of garlic, crushed
2 inch piece of ginger root, crushed
½ teaspoon turmeric powder
½ teaspoon cayenne pepper
2 teaspoons coriander powder
salt to taste
2 medium tomatoes, chopped
1 teaspoon *garam masala* powder (see page 16)
4 cups boiled chickpeas
3 dried tamarinds soaked in water (see page 21)
4 small potatoes, boiled, peeled and cubed (optional)

For Garnish:

1 large onion, chopped
2 fresh green chilies, seeded and chopped
2 lemons, quartered
a few coriander or fresh mint leaves

Heat oil. Add the cumin seeds and grated onions. Cook for just a few minutes. Add crushed garlic and ginger. Cook for 5 minutes on low heat. Add a dash of water, if necessary, so that it doesn't stick to pan. Then add turmeric, coriander, cayenne pepper and salt. Stir and add the chopped tomatoes and *garam masala* powder. Let this spicy mixture cook until the oil separates. Then add the chickpeas and tamarind water. Cook for a while. Add the potatoes (optional). Sprinkle onions and green chilies on top and put lemon wedges and coriander leaves on sides of dish.

Serves: 6

Steamed Rice and Bean Cakes I *(Dhokla)*

These cakes are savory sponge cakes with a spicy, light taste.

2 cups dried red kidney beans
2 cups rice
1 inch piece of ginger root
2 fresh green chilies, seeded
salt to taste
½ cup yogurt
pinch of baking powder

Soak beans and rice overnight in separate bowls. Drain the rice. Wash the skins off the beans. See page 19 for instructions on grinding. Grind beans and rice together in a blender.

Grind the ginger root and chilies.

Combine the two mixtures with salt, yogurt and baking powder. Pour into greased cake tins and steam. Any metal pot deeper than the cake tin will do. Put a trivet at the bottom of the bigger pan, water to come to the level of the trivet. Put the cake tin, covered, on the trivet and a lid on top of the bigger pan. Let it cook in the steam about 25 minutes.

When cool, cut into squares.

Steamed Rice and Bean Cakes II *(Dhokla)*

1 cup rice flour
1 cup red kidney beans
hot water to cover
1 tablespoon yogurt
salt to taste
1 teaspoon turmeric powder
1 teaspoon cayenne pepper
a pinch of asafetida
1 teaspoon whole mustard seeds
2 tablespoons oil or *ghee*
1 fresh green chili, seeded and chopped
a few curry leaves

Soak flour and beans separately in hot water overnight. Wash skins off beans after soaking. Drain. Grind together flour, beans, yogurt, salt, turmeric, cayenne pepper and a pinch of asafetida to form a paste. Steam the paste in 2 large greased baking dishes (see preceding recipe). Fry the mustard seeds in oil until they pop. Add green chili and curry leaves. Fry 1 minute. Pour over the *dhoklas* when ready. Remove from the baking dishes and cut into squares. Serve with coconut chutney.

Serves: 12

Plain Rice Cakes *(Plain Idli)*

This is a good dish to serve instead of rice or bread. The cakes are easy to make.

2½ cups rice
1¼ cup *urad dal*
salt to taste
1 teaspoon black peppercorns, coarsely crushed
pinch of asafetida

Wash and soak rice and *urad dal* separately for about 3 hours or longer. Grind the *urad dal* into a smooth paste and the rice into a coarse paste with a little water. Use the blender. Combine the two mixtures plus salt and spices.

Leave the mixture overnight in a warm place to ferment and rise in a covered container. The next morning, steam the rice cakes in greased *idli* molds or an egg poacher for 5 minutes. Mung beans can be used instead of *urad dal*.

The fermenting makes the *idlis* light and a bit sour. Observe that no rising agent like yeast or baking powder is added.

Yields: 18 cakes

Steamed Rice Cakes *(Masala Idli)*

These are very popular in South India for breakfast. They look like white sponge cakes.

1 cup *urad dal*
¼ cup dried peas
a pinch of asafetida
2½ cups rice
2 tablespoons fresh grated coconut (optional)
2 fresh green chilies, seeded and chopped
a few coriander leaves, chopped
1 inch piece of ginger root, ground
salt to taste
dash of ground black pepper
water to make a paste

Wash and soak the *urad dal* and dried peas for 3 hours. Drain.
Add asafetida and grind thoroughly, adding as little water as needed.

Wash the rice and spread it to dry in a warm oven. When all the moisture is out of the rice, let it cool and grind it coarsely. You should have 2 cups.

Mix 2 cups of ground rice with the pea mixture. Add the other ingredients with enough water to form a thick paste. Let it stand overnight, covered, to ferment.

Grease an egg poacher and put the mixture in it or use an *idli* mold. Serve hot or cold.

Serves: 8

Basic Rice Pancake I *(Dosa)*

Rice pancakes are very popular in South India. They can be eaten hot with any kind of chutney or pickle.

1½ cups rice
½ cup *urad dal*
water to cover
salt to taste
oil to fry
enough water added the next day to form a thick batter

Soak rice and *urad dal* separately for 6 hours. Grind the rice coarsely and the *urad dal* finely (see page 19 for instructions). Mix together, add salt. Keep it covered on the kitchen counter overnight. Before frying, add water to obtain a thick batter-like consistency.

Heat a greased round, flat pan, a heavy *tawa* or a teflon frying pan and pour in 1 to 2 tablespoons of batter. To prevent sticking pour a little oil around the edges. Cover and cook the *dosa* on one side and then flip it over. Brown on both sides.

Yields: 8-10 pancakes

Note: the batter can be frozen in a plastic container for future use. Thaw about 2 hours before using.

Spicy Filling for Rice Pancakes:

1 tablespoon oil
½ teaspoon mustard seeds
½ teaspoon yellow split peas
1 medium onion, chopped
½ teaspoon turmeric powder
salt to taste
½ teaspoon cayenne pepper
2 large potatoes, boiled, peeled and coarsely mashed

Heat oil and add mustard seeds, split peas, onions, turmeric, salt and cayenne pepper and fry for 5 minutes. Add potatoes and mix well.

Place about 1 tablespoon of filling on each pancake. Fold in half and serve hot with coconut chutney.

Quick Rice Pancakes II *(Dosa)*

These are like salty crepes. They can be eaten with a potato filling or with a chutney. They are easy to fix and very nutritious.

2 cups semolina (Cream of Wheat)
½ cup all-purpose white flour *or*
    ½ cup rice flour
½ cup yogurt
salt to taste
enough water to make a thick batter

Mix all the above ingredients and let rest for 1 hour. Fry pancakes on a hot greased griddle.

Serves: 4-6

Instant Pancakes III *(Dosa)*

1 cup all purpose white flour
1 cup semolina (Cream of Wheat)
salt to taste
2 cups buttermilk
1 tablespoon oil
1 teaspoon mustard seeds
2 fresh green chilies, seeded and chopped
a pinch of asafetida
½ cup water
sufficient oil for frying

Sift the flour and combine with semolina, salt and buttermilk to make a batter.

Heat 1 tablespoon of oil and fry mustard seeds till they pop. Then add green chilies and fry for 1 minute more. Pour into the batter and add asafetida along with ½ cup of water.

Heat an iron griddle or a teflon pan. Put a teaspoon of oil on it. Pour some batter on the griddle with a large ladle. Quickly spread the batter evenly into a thin layer. Let it cook for 2 minutes. Pour another teaspoon of oil around the pancake. When cooked on one side, turn over and cook on the other side. Serve the *dosa* with coconut chutney, melted butter, *ghee,* mango or lemon pickle.

Serves: 8

Bombay Cereal *(Poha)*

This salty, savory cereal is a Bombay and Maharastrin favorite. It is served at breakfast time with pickles and a slice of lemon.

1½ cups rice flakes
2 medium potatoes, peeled *or*
   1 cup peas
2 tablespoons *ghee*
2 medium onions, chopped very fine
a few fresh coriander leaves
1 teaspoon cumin seeds
1 teaspoon mustard seeds
a pinch of asafetida
1 teaspoon turmeric powder
salt to taste

Wash and drain the rice flakes. Put aside. Chop the potatoes very fine and soak them in water to cover. Heat *ghee* in a pan and brown onions. Add all other ingredients except the rice flakes. Cook on a low flame until the vegetables are cooked. Add the rice flakes, cover and cook for another 10 minutes.

Serves: 6

Salty Cereal *(Oopma)*

This salty porridge is very popular in South India. It can be eaten any time of the day, served hot or cold. Many eat it instead of dinner at night.

4 tablespoons oil
6 curry leaves (optional)
2 tablespoons *urad dal* (optional)
2 teaspoons yellow split peas
1 teaspoon mustard seeds
2 teaspoons ginger root, finely chopped
2 dried red chilies, crumbled
1 fresh green chili, seeded and chopped
2 cups water
2 cups semolina (Cream of Wheat)
salt to taste
½ cup fried cashews *or*
    ½ cup fried peanuts
juice of 1 lemon
½ cup cooked green peas (optional)

In a heavy saucepan, heat the oil and add the curry leaves, stirring constantly. Add *urad dal* (optional), split peas and mustard seeds. Fry for 1 minute, then add ginger root, red and green chilies. Fry 1-2 minutes more.

Add water. Bring to a boil. Add semolina and salt. Cook in a covered saucepan about 8 minutes. When water is absorbed, mix in cashews, lemon juice and green peas.

Serves: 6-8

Water Puffs (Gol Gappas or Paani Puri)

The puffs without their fillings can be prepared a few days in advance.

Puffs:

    ¾ cup semolina (Cream of Wheat)
    ¾ cup all purpose white flour
    1 tablespoon *urad dal* flour
    ¼ cup warm water, approximately
    ghee or oil for frying

Filling:

    3 cups chickpeas, boiled
    4 potatoes, boiled, peeled and cubed
    ¼ cup ginger chutney (see page 164)

For the Puffs:

Sift the first three ingredients together. Add enough warm water to make a soft dough. Keep kneading for about 20 minutes so that the flours are well blended. Cover with a damp muslin cloth and set aside for half an hour. Uncover and knead again for a few minutes.

Divide dough into four equal parts. On a lightly floured surface roll out each piece as thin as possible. Cut out small rounds with a biscuit cutter, about 1½ inches in diameter. Another method, used more frequently, is to divide the dough into small marble-sized balls and roll each separately. Place the rolled out dough between two layers of damp cloth until all are finished.

Deep-fry 4 at a time until they puff up and are golden brown. Drain them on a paper towel. Cool them completely and store in a large airtight container. The puffs which don't rise should be discarded or used for something else.

To Insert the Filling:

To serve these, make a hole on top of each puff. Fill the hollow of each with 4 boiled chickpeas, 4 small pieces of boiled potato and ½ teaspoon of chutney.

Quickly dip these into cumin water (the recipe follows). These should not be stored on a plate but popped into the mouth immediately.

Yields: 50-60 puffs

Cumin Water *(Zeera Pani or Jal Jeera)*

This can be served as an appetizer by itself, particularly in the summertime. Remember, it is hot and tangy.

8 oz. seedless tamarind
6 pints of water
2 teaspoons fresh mint *or*
  1 teaspoon dried mint
6 teaspoons salt
8 teaspoons black salt *
1 tablespoon ground fresh ginger root
2 tablespoons ground cumin seeds
6 teaspoons sugar
1 teaspoon *garam masala* powder (see page 16)
2 teaspoons cayenne pepper
¼ cup lemon juice
1 tray ice cubes
a few sprigs of fresh mint, for garnish
lemon slices, for garnish

Wash and soak the tamarind in water overnight. Strain it, pressing down on the pulp. Throw away the pulp. Save the water.

Combine the next 8 ingredients. Add to the tamarind water. Mix well and set aside for about three hours to blend flavors. Strain through a damp muslin cloth. Add lemon juice and ice to the liquid. Add more sugar if it tastes sour. If it is too strong, dilute it with more water. Serve with more ice and decorate with a few sprigs of mint leaves or lemon slices. Stir well each time you serve it.

This keeps for about 3 or 4 days in the refrigerator.

*Black salt should be available at Indian grocery stores. For instructions on grinding, see page 19.

Plain Fried Crackers *(Matthi)*

2 cups white flour
salt to taste
2 teaspoons peppercorns, coarsely crushed
½ teaspoon of carom seeds
½ cup oil or *ghee*
¼ to ½ cup of water

Combine the flour, salt, peppercorns, carom seeds and oil to form a crumbly mixture. Make a stiff dough by adding water.

Roll out into small 3 inch rounds and deep-fry over low heat **till** the crackers turn a pale golden brown.

Cool and store in an airtight container. These can be stored for over a month.

Yields: 12 to 14 crackers

Fried Curried Rice Crackers *(Murukku)*

This is a very popular snack from Madras, delicious in the morning with a cup of coffee.

2 teaspoons cumin seeds
1 cup chickpea flour
salt to taste
1 teaspoon cayenne pepper
1 teaspoon baking powder
pinch of asafetida
¼ to ½ cup water
4 tablespoons oil
3 cups rice flour
2 cups oil for frying

Roast cumin seeds, crush and add to the chickpea flour. Add salt, cayenne and baking powder.

Dissolve asafetida in about ½-¼ cup of water.

Add oil to the rice flour with your fingertips or a fork.

Combine the chickpea flour mixture and the rice flour mixture. Make a stiff dough with asafetida water.

Press dough through a pastry tube or cookie press to make ring shapes, dropping them into the hot oil. Fry till golden. Remove and drain.

Yields: 20-25 crackers

Curried Fried Noodles *(Sev)*

1 cup chickpea flour
½ teaspoon cumin seeds
½ teaspoon salt
½ teaspoon cayenne pepper
1 teaspoon oil
¼ cup water for mixing
2 cups oil for frying

Mix all the dry ingredients together. Rub in 1 teaspoon oil and add water to make a stiff dough.

Pass through a large-holed sieve (or use a cookie press) into the hot oil to make snake-shaped, crisp noodles. Fry golden brown and drain on a paper towel. Repeat the process until all the dough is used.

Cool and break into 1 inch pieces. Store in an airtight container. We serve these in small bowls with cocktails.

Yields: several small bowls

Savory Mixture *(Chiwda or Chivra)*

1 tablespoon raisins
½ dried coconut
¼ teaspoon turmeric powder
½ cup oil for frying
2 tablespoons peanuts, raw or roasted
2 tablespoons cashew nuts
1 cup rice flakes
2 fresh green chilies, seeded
1 teaspoon salt
¼ teaspoon cayenne pepper
2 teaspoons sugar
¼ teaspoon mustard seeds
1 teaspoon lemon juice
a few curry leaves

Wash and dry raisins. Thinly slice the coconut and sprinkle turmeric over it. Fry the coconut and raisins until they are crisp. Drain on a paper towel.

Using the remaining oil, fry the nuts till golden brown and drain on a paper towel. Fry the rice flakes and mix in all the other ingredients. Fry until the mixture is dry. Drain on a paper towel. Let cool completely before storing in an airtight container. Keeps fresh for 2-3 weeks.

This is good to munch on with beer or whiskey.

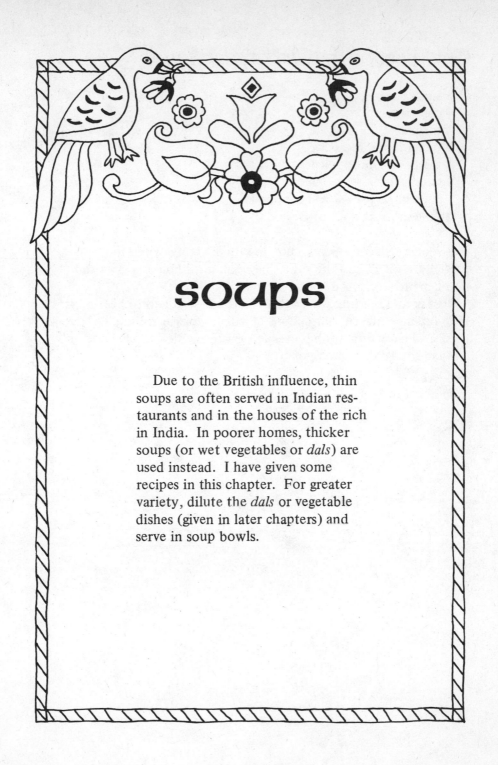

soups

Due to the British influence, thin soups are often served in Indian restaurants and in the houses of the rich in India. In poorer homes, thicker soups (or wet vegetables or *dals*) are used instead. I have given some recipes in this chapter. For greater variety, dilute the *dals* or vegetable dishes (given in later chapters) and serve in soup bowls.

Cold Beet Soup *(Chukandar Soup)*

6 small beets
4 cups water
salt to taste
2 tablespoons sugar
1 teaspoon lemon juice
1 cup yogurt
1 cucumber, peeled and chopped
2 tablespoons chopped fresh dill

Peel and halve the beets. Boil in salted water. When they are partially cooked, add the sugar and cook until tender. Cool and puree in blender. Add lemon juice and chill.

Just before serving, stir yogurt vigorously and add to beet mixture. Save out a couple of tablespoons of yogurt for garnishing. Mix well. Pour into individual soup bowls and garnish with chopped cucumber, dill and a drop of beaten yogurt.

Serves: 6

Cabbage and Potato Soup *(Sabzi Ka Soup)*

This thick soup tastes wonderful on a cold winter's night served with whole wheat bread, butter and cheese.

2 teaspoons vegetable oil
1 medium cabbage, shredded
1 medium raw potato, chopped
4 cups of hot water
1 cup milk
salt and pepper to taste

Heat the oil. Saute a little cabbage for garnish and set aside.

In the same oil, saute the rest of the cabbage and add chopped potato. Add hot water, cover and simmer gently for 20 minutes or until the potato is tender.

Mash and press the soup through a strainer or food mill, or use a blender. Then add milk, salt and pepper. Heat thoroughly but do not boil. Grind black pepper on top. Garnish with fried cabbage and serve.

Serves: 6

Carrot Soup *(Gajjar Soup)*

Children love this soup.

3 cups raw carrots, diced
2 medium tomatoes
2 teaspoons oil
2 medium onions, chopped
2 cloves garlic, minced
6 cups milk
½ cup water
salt and pepper to taste
½ cup sour cream, for garnish
a few fresh parsley leaves, chopped, for garnish

Cook the carrots in a small amount of water until soft. Drain the water and mash the carrots. Blanch fresh tomatoes in boiling water, peel and chop finely. Saute tomatoes in oil and add onions and garlic. Fry till wilted, but do not brown. Add the carrot puree and mix well. Gradually add the milk and water and heat thoroughly, but do not boil. Season to taste. Serve in individual bowls with a dollop of sour cream and chopped parsley.

Serves: 8

Spinach Soup *(Paalak Soup)*

4 cups water
1 lb. fresh spinach
salt to taste
a dash of black pepper
1 tablespoon oil
1 teaspoon cumin seeds
2 medium onions, chopped
2 teaspoons lemon juice
½ cup sour cream

Bring water to a boil. Add spinach, salt and pepper. When spinach is cooked, pour into a blender and puree it.

Heat the oil in a saucepan and fry the cumin seeds until they puff up. Add the onions and fry till wilted. Add the puree and heat thoroughly. Remove from heat, stir in the lemon juice and sour cream.

Serves: 6

Curried Tomato Soup *(Tamatar Soup)*

8 medium tomatoes, chopped
2 medium onions, chopped
salt to taste
4 cups water
1 cup milk
2 teaspoons cornstarch
dash of pepper
2 teaspoons sugar
6 lemon wedges, for garnish

Simmer tomatoes and onions in salted water until vegetables are soft. Strain or put through a food mill. Discard residue. Add milk mixed with cornstarch. Cook until mixture thickens. Remove from heat. Add pepper and sugar. Serve with lemon wedges.

Serves: 6

Tomato Soup *(Tamatar Soup)*

This is good as a first course or as a late night hot drink.

1 tablespoon vegetable oil
½ teaspoon cumin seeds
6 whole peppercorns
2 medium onions, diced
1 teaspoon all purpose white flour
8 medium tomatoes, chopped
1 bay leaf
salt to taste
4 cups water
fried bread cubes *or*
    6 tablespoons boiled rice

Heat the oil, add cumin seeds and peppercorns. Fry till seeds puff
up and the cumin seeds change color. Add the onions and saute them.
Add flour, chopped tomatoes, bay leaf, salt and water. Bring to a
boil and simmer for 20 minutes. Remove from heat and put through
a strainer or food mill. Serve with fried bread cubes or a tablespoon
of boiled rice in large mugs or bowls.

Serves: 6

Mulligatawny Soup *(Dal Soup)*

An authentic Indian soup.

1 tablespoon oil
1 teaspoon cumin seeds
2 medium onions, sliced
½ teaspoon turmeric powder
1 cup yellow split peas *or*
   1 cup red lentils, washed
6 cups water
salt to taste
¼ teaspoon cayenne pepper
½ teaspoon ground black pepper
1 tablespoon lemon juice
12 tablespoons boiled white rice
a few chopped mint leaves, for garnish

Heat the oil. Add cumin seeds and onions and fry till the cumin changes color. Add the turmeric powder and yellow split peas. Fry 1 minute. Add the water, salt, cayenne and black pepper. Bring to a boil and simmer for 30 minutes or until the yellow split peas are tender. Strain them. Add lemon juice to the strained fluid. Use the strained lentils for another dish or discard them.

To serve, put 2 tablespoons of rice in each bowl and pour the soup over the rice. Garnish with chopped fresh mint leaves.

Serves: 6

South Indian Soup *(Rassam)*

1 tablespoon tamarind
1 cup water
¼ cup pigeon peas *or*
   ¼ cup red lentils *or* green lentils
2 cups water
4 cloves garlic
2 teaspoons peppercorns
1 teaspoon cumin seeds
2 dried red chilies
salt to taste
2 medium tomatoes, chopped

Baghar (see page 18):

2 teaspoons oil
½ teaspoon mustard seeds
curry leaves *or* bay leaves

Soak tamarind in water for 1 hour. Strain it and discard the pulp. Set aside.

Wash pigeon peas and boil in water for about 25 minutes or until tender. Set aside.

Crush the garlic and peppercorns coarsely. Add these to the tamarind water along with cumin seeds, broken red chilies and salt. Boil for 10 minutes. Add the chopped tomatoes and cooked lentils. Boil for 5 minutes longer.

Make the *baghar* and pour over the soup. Stir and serve.

Serves: 6

Curried Soup *(Karhi)*

This is a sour, thick soup.

½ cup chickpea flour
1 teaspoon turmeric powder
1 cup yogurt *or*
   2 cups buttermilk
1 teaspoon cayenne pepper
½ teaspoon sugar
salt to taste
4 cups warm water
1 fresh green chili, seeded and sliced

Baghar (see page 18):

2 tablespoons oil
1 teaspoon cumin seeds
1 teaspoon mustard seeds
1 teaspoon fenugreek seeds
pinch of asafetida

20 *pakoras* (see pages 29-34)
a few coriander leaves, chopped, for garnish

In a heavy bottomed saucepan combine the first 7 ingredients.
Cook for 15-20 minutes, stirring constantly. Add the green chilies.
When the soup is thick, turn off the heat and add the *baghar*. Stir.
Add the *pakoras*. Serve with rice and garnish with chopped coriander
leaves.

Serves: 8

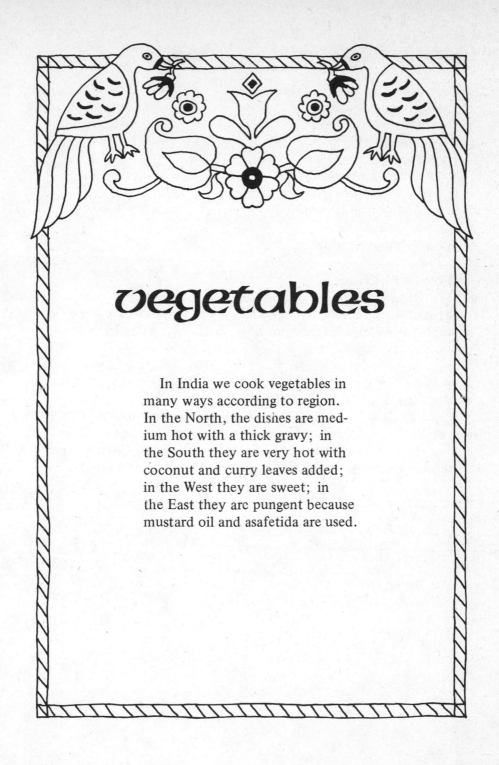

vegetables

In India we cook vegetables in
many ways according to region.
In the North, the dishes are medium hot with a thick gravy; in
the South they are very hot with
coconut and curry leaves added;
in the West they are sweet; in
the East they are pungent because
mustard oil and asafetida are used.

Cabbage Rolls

1 medium-sized head of cabbage
2 raw potatoes, peeled
2 medium onions
2 tablespoons oil
1 teaspoon ginger paste
4 cloves garlic, chopped
½ teaspoon turmeric powder
½ teaspoon cayenne pepper
½ teaspoon anise seed
½ teaspoon mango powder
salt to taste
½ cup oil for frying

Separate 10 large cabbage leaves and set aside. Shred the remaining cabbage. Finely chop the potatoes. Slice 1 onion and grind the other.

Heat 2 tablespoons oil and brown the sliced and ground onions with ginger and garlic. Add all the spices, shredded cabbage, potatoes and salt. Cook on low heat until tender and dry.

Spoon the mixture into each large cabbage leaf and fold it like a parcel. Tie with a heavy thread to prevent re-opening. Heat the ½ cup oil in a shallow skillet and fry the rolls till golden. Cover the pan and cook till cabbage is tender. Remove threads before serving.

Serves: 8-10

Savory Semolina with Cabbage and Other Vegetables *(Rawa Oopma)*

This is quite thick, like a rice dish.

½ cup cabbage, shredded
1 carrot, cubed
½ cup green peas
water to cover
6 tablespoons oil or *ghee*, divided
1 cup semolina (Cream of Wheat)
½ teaspoon mustard seeds
1 teaspoon *urad dal*
1 teaspoon yellow split peas
2 fresh green chilies, seeded and chopped
2 medium onions, chopped
salt to taste
pinch of turmeric powder
6 curry leaves, fresh or dried
¼ cup cashews, fried
3 teaspoons lemon juice
coriander leaves, for garnish

Cook the cabbage, carrot and peas in water to cover. When they are soft, set aside.

Heat 2 tablespoons oil and fry the semolina, stirring, until it is lightly roasted. Set aside.

In a saucepan make a *baghar* out of 2 tablespoons of oil, mustard seeds, *urad dal* and yellow split peas. Fry till the mustard seeds pop. Add the green chilies, onions, salt, turmeric and curry leaves. When the onions are light brown, set aside.

Drain the vegetables. Add sufficient water, if necessary, to make 1½ cups. Add this vegetable stock to the *baghar*. Bring this to a boil.

Add the semolina slowly, stirring. Add the remaining oil or *ghee* and cook, covered, for two more minutes. Check to see if more water is needed. If so, add a little. Remove from heat.

Add the cashews and lemon juice and stir. Garnish with coriander leaves. Serve hot.

Serves: 8

Fried Green Chilies *(Tali Hari Mirchi)*

These chilies are very hot. Please eat a little yogurt with them.

12 fresh green chilies
1 teaspoon turmeric powder
1 teaspoon cayenne pepper
2 teaspoons coriander powder
salt to taste
2 tablespoons brown sugar
2 tablespoons chickpea flour
2 tablespoons oil
½ teaspoon carom seeds
½ teaspoon cumin seeds
½ cup oil, for frying

Wash the chilies and slit one side of each. Remove the seeds and wash well. Mix all the other ingredients except the oil, and fill the chilies.

Heat the oil and fry them until they are cooked.

Serves: 12

Hyderabadi Chili Curry

This also is very hot.

½ cup oil
8 large, fresh green chilies
6 medium onions, chopped
1 teaspoon garlic paste or powder
1 teaspoon ginger paste or powder
2 tablespoons ground, roasted sesame seed
1 teaspoon cumin seeds
2 teaspoons coriander seeds
2 tablespoons ground raw peanuts
½ cup tamarind juice
salt to taste

Heat oil in a heavy skillet. Slit the chilies lengthwise, remove seeds and fry till brown. Remove from oil, drain and set aside.

In the same oil fry the onions. When the onions are nicely browned, add garlic, ginger, sesame, cumin, coriander and peanuts. Fry for about 5 minutes. Add the tamarind juice and salt. Cook for another 10 minutes. Then add the fried chilies and cook for another 10 minutes.

Serves: 8

Curried Corn (Makki Ki Sabzi)

3 tablespoons oil
1 teaspoon mustard seeds
4 medium onions, sliced
1 teaspoon ground garlic
1 teaspoon turmeric powder
1 teaspoon cayenne pepper
2 teaspoons coriander powder
2½ cup water, divided
1 teaspoon chopped ginger root
1 cup yogurt
salt to taste
10 ears of corn, grated
2 teaspoons lemon juice
1 teaspoon *garam masala* powder
1 fresh green chili, seeded and sliced, for garnish
a few coriander leaves, chopped, for garnish

Heat the oil in a wok and add the mustard seeds. Fry till they pop and then add the onions. Fry till they turn golden.

Mix the garlic and the three spices in a small bowl with ½ cup water. Add to the wok and cook about 5 minutes.

Add the ginger, yogurt, salt and corn. Cook 5 minutes more, stirring. Add 2 more cups of water gradually and cook 20 minutes. When corn is very soft, turn off the heat. Pour in lemon juice and mix in *garam masala* powder. Garnish with chilies and coriander leaves.

Serves: 10

Fried Eggplant *(Tale Baigan)*

This is absolutely delicious.

2 medium eggplants
salt and black pepper

Batter:

    ½ cup chickpea flour
    ½ cup yogurt
    salt to taste
    1 teaspoon cayenne pepper
    1 teaspoon garlic powder or paste
    1 teaspoon cumin seeds
    2 cups oil for frying

Slice the eggplant ¼ inch thick, sprinkle with salt and pepper and set aside. Make a batter with the chickpea flour, yogurt, salt, cayenne, garlic and cumin seeds. Dip the eggplant slices in the batter and deep-fry. Serve with mint chutney and *chappatis.*

Serves: 4-6

Mashed Curried Eggplant I
(Baigan Ka Bharta)

This is a very popular dish of Punjab and Rajasthan. The chopped raw onions give this dish texture. We serve this with hot buttered *chappatis*—using the *chappatis* as pincers to enclose the eggplant mixture. The yogurt gives this a richer taste than the following recipe.

3 medium eggplants
3 tablespoons oil
1 medium onion, sliced
4 cloves garlic, crushed
2 medium onions, ground
1 teaspoon turmeric powder
salt to taste
½ cup yogurt
2 teaspoons *garam masala* powder
1 fresh green chili, seeded and chopped
2 teaspoons mango powder
1 medium onion, chopped

Make a slit in each eggplant and roast them in a 450 degree oven till soft. Peel and mash them.

In a saucepan heat the oil. Add the sliced onion and fry till it is wilted. Add the garlic and ground onions and fry till they are wilted. Add the turmeric, salt and yogurt. Cook 2-3 minutes.

Add the mashed eggplant, *garam masala* powder, green chili and mango powder. Cook for 5-10 minutes and keep stirring.

Remove from heat. Add the raw onions and stir.

Serves: 8

Mashed Curried Eggplant II
(Baigan Bharta)

This is hotter than the preceeding recipe.

4 medium eggplants
4 large onions, peeled
1 tablespoon oil
1 teaspoon cumin seeds
1 fresh green chili, seeded and chopped
1 teaspoon curry powder
salt to taste
1 teaspoon lemon juice
1 teaspoon *garam masala* powder

Bake the eggplant and whole onions in the oven for 25 minutes or until tender. Peel the eggplant and coarsely mash the pulp. Chop the onions.

Heat oil and add cumin seeds and chopped onions. Fry 2 minutes. Add the eggplant, chili, curry powder and salt. Cook for 5 minutes. Remove from heat and add lemon juice and *garam masala.*

Serves: 8

Note: For variations, mashed potatoes, pumpkin, or watermelon may be used in place of the eggplant to make this recipe.

Eggplant Cooked with Whole Spices
(Sabat Masala Ke Baigan)

The eggplant in this recipe is not mashed, but cut in 2 inch cubes. The spices are deliberately left coarse so that you distinguish each individual flavor.

1 medium eggplant
3 tablespoons oil
a pinch of asafetida
1 teaspoon cumin seeds
1 tablespoon coriander seeds, coarsely ground
3 dried red chilies, coarsely ground
1 teaspoon turmeric powder
salt to taste
2 teaspoons mango powder

Cut the unpeeled eggplant into 2 inch cubes and cover with cold water. Set aside.

Heat the oil in a wok. When hot, remove from burner and add asafetida and cumin seeds.

Drain the eggplant then put the wok back on the burner and add the eggplant. Add the coriander seeds, red chili, turmeric and salt. Cover and cook until done. Take off the stove and add mango powder. Stir.

Serves: 6-8

Whole Eggplant Curry
(Hyderabadi Saare Baigan)

This has a thick sauce with the flavor of tomatoes, peanuts and coconut predominating.

2 tablespoons ground roasted peanuts
¼ dried coconut, roasted and ground
1 teaspoon ground roasted cumin seeds
1 teaspoon ground roasted fenugreek seeds
1 teaspoon ground ginger root
1 teaspoon ground garlic
1 teaspoon cayenne pepper
1 teaspoon turmeric powder
2 teaspoons coriander powder
2 onions, grated and fried in a little oil

Baghar:

6 tablespoons oil
½ teaspoon cumin seeds
½ teaspoon fenugreek seeds

4 small eggplants, cut in half
salt to taste
4 tomatoes, chopped

Combine the first 10 ingredients in a bowl. Set aside.
Heat the oil in a wok and add cumin and fenugreek. Fry 2-3 minutes. Add the halved eggplant. Cover the pan and cook 10 minutes.
Add the salt, tomatoes and the first 10 ingredients you have set aside. Stir. Cover and simmer 20 minutes or until eggplant is tender.

Serves: 6-8

Stuffed Eggplant *(Bharwa Baigan I)*

4 small eggplants
1 teaspoon turmeric powder
2 teaspoons coriander powder
1 teaspoon cayenne pepper
½ teaspoon fenugreek seeds, finely ground
1 teaspoon mango powder
1 teaspoon sugar
salt to taste
1 medium onion, grated
¼ cup water
4 tablespoons oil for frying

Wash and dry the eggplants. Make four deep slits lengthwise, being careful not to cut completely through. Mix the rest of the ingredients except the oil, with water. Stuff paste inside the slits of the eggplant and fry in hot oil in a wok on slow flame. When done on one side, turn over and cook on the other side. Remove when tender. Serve 1 eggplant to a person.

Serves: 4

Horseradish Curry *(Muli Ka Keema)*

This is hot in taste, dry in texture.

2 tablespoons *ghee* or oil
1 teaspoon cumin seeds
4 medium onions, grated
2 cups grated white horseradish
2 dried red chilies, crushed
6 cloves garlic, crushed
salt to taste
a few chopped green coriander leaves
½ cup crushed roasted peanuts
2 teaspoons mango powder
2 teaspoons *garam masala* powder

In a wok, heat the *ghee* and fry the cumin seeds till they darken slightly, then add the onions and fry till they are light brown.

Add the horseradish, chilies, garlic, salt and coriander leaves. Cook for about 20 minutes until the horseradish is done.

Add the peanuts, mango powder and *garam masala*. Simmer 10 minutes more.

Serves: 6-8

Green Mango Curry *(Kairee Ki Sabzi)*

This is a sweet-sour curry which you would eat in small quantities.

6 green mangoes
water to cover
3 tablespoons oil
4 medium onions, chopped
1 teaspoon garlic paste or powder
1 teaspoon fenugreek seeds
2 teaspoons cayenne pepper
1 teaspoon turmeric powder
3 teaspoons coriander powder
½ cup hot water
salt to taste
2 tablespoons brown sugar

Peel each mango and cut into 4 pieces. Discard the pits. Boil in water to cover until tender. Drain.

Heat the oil in a wok or skillet and brown the onions. Add the spices and ½ cup hot water and simmer for 5 minutes.

Add the mangoes, salt and sugar. Cook until the mixture thickens.

Serves: 12

Green Peas and Cheese Curry *(Matar Paneer)*

Paneer:

    4 cups milk
    2 tablespoons lemon juice
    ¼ cup *ghee* or oil for frying

Curry:

    3 tablespoons oil
    1 teaspoon cumin seeds
    4 medium onions, ground
    ½ cup hot water
    1 teaspoon garlic powder
    1 teaspoon ginger powder
    4 teaspoons tomato puree
    1 teaspoon turmeric powder
    1½ teaspoons cayenne pepper
    3 teaspoons coriander powder
    salt to taste
    1 cup yogurt, beaten
    1 cup peas, cooked
    1 teaspoon *garam masala* powder
    coriander leaves, chopped, for garnish

Make the *paneer* (see page 20) and cut in 1 inch cubes. Fry in *ghee* until light gold in color.

In a wok or skillet, heat the oil. Add the cumin seeds and fry 2 minutes. Add the onions and fry till brown. Add ½ cup hot water, garlic and ginger and simmer for 5 minutes.

Add the tomato puree, spices and salt. Stir and cook a few minutes.

Add the yogurt and simmer 10 minutes more. Then add the peas and *garam masala* powder.

Before serving add the *paneer*. Stir gently. Garnish with coriander leaves.

Serves: 8-10

Whole Spice Vegetable Curry
(Sabat Masala Sabzi)

This curry is very pleasing to the eye. The potatoes and cauliflower are yellow and the peas are green.

3 tablespoons oil
1 teaspoon cumin seeds
1 teaspoon mustard seeds
3 medium raw potatoes, peeled and chopped
1 cup raw green peas
½ raw cauliflower, chopped
¼ cup water
1 teaspoon turmeric powder
1 teaspoon crushed dried red chili
2 teaspoons crushed coriander seeds
1 teaspoon crushed ginger
1 teaspoon crushed garlic
1 teaspoon *garam masala* powder
1 teaspoon mango powder *or*
   1 teaspoon lemon juice
salt to taste

Heat oil in a wok. Add cumin and mustard seeds. Fry 2 minutes. Add the potatoes, peas, cauliflower and the rest of the ingredients. Cover with a lid and simmer 20 minutes. Uncover and keep simmering for 5 minutes. Stir so that it doesn't stick to the bottom of the pan.

Serves: 12

Green Pea Curry *(Matar Ki Sabzi)*

This has a sauce of onions and peas.

2 tablespoons *ghee* or oil
1 teaspoon cumin seeds
2 medium onions, sliced
4 medium onions, ground
3 tomatoes, chopped
1 teaspoon turmeric powder
1 teaspoon cayenne pepper
2 teaspoons coriander powder
1 tablespoon sugar
3 cups of peas, fresh or frozen
salt to taste
½ cup hot water
1 teaspoon *garam masala* powder
1 tablespoon lemon juice
lots of chopped coriander leaves, for garnish

In a heavy skillet, heat the *ghee* or oil and add cumin seeds. Fry 2 minutes. Add sliced onions and brown them. Add ground onions and fry till they are tender. Add tomatoes, all the powdered spices and sugar. Next add the peas, salt and hot water and cook for 10 minutes. Add *garam masala* powder, lemon juice and garnish with chopped coriander leaves.

Serves: 8

Stuffed Bell Peppers *(Bharwa Simla Mirch)*

The mung bean filling gives these a very different taste from the western version of stuffed peppers.

1 cup mung beans
water to cover
4 tablespoons oil, divided
1 teaspoon cumin seeds
1 teaspoon turmeric powder
1 teaspoon cayenne pepper
2 teaspoons coriander powder
1 fresh green chili, seeded and chopped
salt to taste
1/3 cup water
2 medium onions, chopped
2 teaspoons lemon juice
1 teaspoon *garam masala* powder
6 bell peppers

Soak mung beans in water for 3 hours. Drain, grind in blender and set aside.

Heat 2 tablespoons of oil in a frying pan and add cumin, other spices, chilies and salt. Fry a minute or so.

Add the 1/3 cup of water, then the ground mung beans and the chopped onions. Cook and stir for 5 minutes. Remove from heat. Add the lemon juice and *garam masala*. Mix thoroughly and set aside.

Wash the peppers and cut off the tops. Remove the seeds, rinse with cold water and drain. Stuff the peppers with the mung bean mixture.

Heat the remaining oil (2 tablespoons) in a wok. Put all the peppers in the wok and fry them on all sides over medium heat. If the oil splatters, cover the pan. When the peppers are done, take them out and cut in half to serve.

They may be baked, instead of fried, in a 350 degree oven for 20 minutes.

Serves: 12

Dry Curried Potatoes with Bell Peppers and Okra *(Aloo, Bhindi and Simla Mirch)*

6 tablespoons oil
2 teaspoons cumin seeds
2 medium onions, thinly sliced
2 medium raw potatoes, peeled and thinly sliced
2 medium peppers, thinly sliced
½ lb. fresh okra, thinly sliced (optional)
2 teaspoons turmeric powder
2 teaspoons cayenne pepper
4 teaspoons coriander powder
salt to taste
2 teaspoons *garam masala* powder
2 teaspoons mango powder

Heat the oil in a wok and fry cumin seeds for 1-2 minutes. Add the sliced onions and fry till wilted.

Add the potatoes, peppers and okra and stir-fry for 15-20 minutes.

Add the powdered spices and salt. Stir, cover and cook 10 minutes. Stir gently, making sure not to break any of the vegetables.

Remove from heat. Add mango powder and *garam masala* powder. Mix well.

Serves: 8

Potatoes and Peas Curry *(Aloo Matar Curry)*

2 tablespoons oil
2 medium onions, sliced
1 teaspoon turmeric powder
1/3 cup water
3 medium raw potatoes, peeled and quartered
1 cup fresh peas or frozen peas
1 fresh green chili, seeded and chopped
salt to taste
1 teaspoon cayenne pepper
2 teaspoons coriander powder
½ cup water
1 teaspoon *garam masala* powder
2 teaspoons lemon juice

Heat oil and brown the onions. Add turmeric and 1/3 cup water.
Fry 1 minute. Add the potatoes, peas and chili. Cook for 5 minutes.
Add salt, cayenne and coriander. Fry 3 minutes.
Pour in ½ cup water, cover with a lid and simmer on low heat.
When potatoes are done, remove from heat, add *garam masala* powder and lemon juice.

Serves: 6-8

use larger potatoes or use ½ spices called for.

Dry Potatoes *(Sookhe Aloo)*

This is one of my favorite recipes. Since the potatoes are fried raw, they have a different texture. It is very tangy.

3 small raw unpeeled potatoes, each cut in half
water to cover
3 tablespoons oil, preferably mustard oil
1 teaspoon cumin seeds
1 onion, sliced
1 teaspoon turmeric powder
3 teaspoons coriander powder
1½ teaspoons cayenne pepper
1 teaspoon cumin powder
salt to taste
1 teaspoon *garam masala* powder
2 teaspoons mango powder

Soak the potatoes in water to cover for 1 hour.

Heat oil in a wok. Add the cumin and sliced onions. Fry till onions are wilted. Drain the potatoes. Add them to the wok. Fry for 10 minutes until crisp.

Add the 4 powdered spices and salt. Cover and cook 10 minutes until potatoes are tender.

Turn off heat. Add the *garam masala* and mango powders. Mix well.

Serves: 8

White Potato Curry *(Safed Aloo)*

Since this curry has no turmeric to turn it yellow, it is white. It's also a mild curry.

3 tablespoons oil
2 teaspoons whole *garam masala*
2 bay leaves
6 onions, ground
12 large raw potatoes, peeled and quartered
2 tablespoons ground poppy seeds
1 tablespoon ground almonds
2 tablespoons ground coconut paste
1 tablespoon ground fresh ginger root
8 cloves garlic, ground
3 whole dried red chilies
2 teaspoons coriander seeds
salt to taste
1 cup yogurt
2 cups milk

Heat the oil. Put in the *garam masala* and bay leaves. Fry 2 minutes.

Add the onions and fry till golden. Then add the potatoes and the rest of the ingredients, save the milk. Mix well. Continue to simmer for 10-15 minutes.

Add the milk, simmer for another 10 minutes.

Serves: 12

Sour Potato Curry *(Khatte Aloo)*

This is very popular in Northeast India. The buttermilk and turmeric together make a lemon-colored sauce.

2 tablespoons oil
1 teaspoon cumin seeds
1 cup buttermilk
1 teaspoon turmeric powder
1½ teaspoons cayenne pepper
3 teaspoons coriander powder
salt to taste
1 cup water
3 potatoes, boiled, peeled and quartered
a few chopped mint or coriander leaves, for garnish

Heat the oil in a wok and add cumin seeds. Fry 1 minute. Set aside.

Mix the next four ingredients in a bowl. Pour this in the wok and cook 10 minutes.

Add salt and water. Simmer for 3-4 minutes. Add the boiled potatoes, stir and turn off heat. Garnish with mint or coriander.

Serves: 6-8

Nepalese Potato Pickle
(Nepali Aloo Ka Achaar)

2 tablespoons sesame seeds
1 tablespoon cumin seeds
¼ cup water
1 teaspoon turmeric powder
salt to taste
1 teaspoon cayenne pepper
2 tablespoons lemon juice
½ cup yogurt, optional
3 medium potatoes, boiled, peeled and sliced
1 tablespoon oil, preferably mustard oil
2 medium onions, sliced
2 fresh green chilies, seeded and halved
1 teaspoon thinly sliced ginger root
pinch of asafetida

Roast the sesame and cumin seeds in a dry pan. Grind in a blender with ¼ cup of water. Place in a bowl and add turmeric, salt, cayenne, lemon juice, yogurt and potatoes. Stir carefully. Set aside.

Heat oil. Fry the onions, chilies, ginger and asafetida till onions are golden. Pour this sauce over the potato mixture and stir.

Chill in the refrigerator. This will keep a week.

Serves: 6-8

Note: Cooked eggplant slices, cabbage wedges or pepper strips can be pickled in the same way.

Nepalese Potatoes *(Nepali Aloo Tareko)*

The combination of oil and *ghee* and the mixture of spices makes this different.

1 tablespoon oil
1 tablespoon *ghee*
½ teaspoon fenugreek seed
2 medium onions, sliced
3 medium raw potatoes, peeled and sliced
4 cloves garlic, crushed
½ teaspoon turmeric powder
1 teaspoon cumin powder
1 fresh green chili, seeded and sliced lengthwise
1 teaspoon coriander powder
1 teaspoon crushed ginger
1 teaspoon cayenne pepper
salt to taste

Heat oil and *ghee*. Fry fenugreek seeds till they pop. Add the onions and potatoes. Fry 5 minutes.

Add all the remaining ingredients, cover and cook over lowest heat, stirring constantly. If necessary add a bit of water. Cover and cook until potatoes are tender.

Serves: 6-8

Spicy Potatoes *(Masala Aloo)*

3 tablespoons oil
3 cloves garlic, chopped
1 dried red chili, crushed
½ teaspoon fenugreek seeds
1 teaspoon cumin seeds
a pinch of asafetida
3 medium raw potatoes, sliced
2 onions, ground
2 cloves garlic, ground
½ teaspoon turmeric powder
1 teaspoon cayenne pepper
½ teaspoon black pepper
2 teaspoons coriander powder
salt to taste
½ cup water

Heat oil in a wok. Stir in garlic, crushed red chili, fenugreek, cumin seed and asafetida. Add sliced potatoes and stir well. Add onions, garlic, all other ground spices, salt and water. Cook until done.

Serves: 6-8

Mashed Curried Potatoes *(Aloo Bharta)*

3 medium potatoes, boiled and peeled
3 medium onions, finely chopped
1 fresh green chili, seeded and chopped
salt to taste
1 teaspoon cayenne pepper
1 tablespoon *masala* and oil from any Indian pickle
2 tablespoons lemon juice
a few mint or coriander leaves, chopped
1 tablespoon oil
1 teaspoon cumin seeds

Mash the potatoes. Add all the other ingredients except the oil and cumin. Set aside.

Heat the oil. Add the cumin seeds and fry for 2 minutes. Add the potato mixture and mix thoroughly. Heat carefully over very low heat.

These can be stuffed inside a *parantha* and then fried.

Serves: 6-8

Steamed Curried Potatoes *(Dam Aloo)*

This has a different taste because the potatoes are not fried. It is milder than the other potato curries.

6-7 medium raw potatoes
2 cups yogurt
4 teaspoons coriander powder
6 medium onions, ground
6 cloves garlic, ground *or*
   1 teaspoon garlic powder
2 teaspoons fresh ground ginger root *or*
   1 teaspoon ginger powder
salt to taste
1 teaspoon turmeric powder
2 teaspoons cayenne pepper
2 teaspoons *garam masala* powder
4 tablespoons *ghee* or oil
a few mint leaves, chopped

Peel and cut each potato in half. Prick each potato several times with a fork. Mix the rest of the ingredients and add to the potatoes.

Cook over low heat in a heavy saucepan with a tight-fitting cover for 20-25 minutes. In a pressure cooker, it will take 10 minutes.

Serves: 12

Stuffed Potatoes *(Bharwa Aloo)*

This is one of my favorite recipes for a party.

6 medium raw potatoes, peeled
8 tablespoons oil, divided
1 teaspoon cumin seeds
2 medium onions, ground
6 cloves garlic, ground
1 teaspoon ground ginger root
1 teaspoon turmeric powder
1 teaspoon cayenne pepper
2 teaspoons coriander powder
1 teaspoon *garam masala,* ground
2 tomatoes, chopped
½ cup yogurt
salt to taste
1 tablespoon raisins
½ teaspoon cloves
a few mint or coriander leaves, for garnish

Cut the top quarter off the potatoes. Keep the tops. Carefully scoop out the center of each potato, using a knife. Save the pulp.

Heat 2 tablespoons of oil. Add cumin, onions and garlic. Cook till onions are golden.

Add all the spices, tomatoes, yogurt and salt. Cook. When the tomatoes are tender, add the raisins and potato pulp. Cook 10-15 minutes more.

Stuff the spice mixture inside the potatoes and cover with the tops of the potatoes. Secure with a toothpick on each potato. Set aside any extra spice mixture.

Heat the remaining 6 tablespoons of oil and add cloves. Fry 1-2 minutes. Add the potatoes, fry and turn them till they are light brown. Cover with a tight lid and cook until they are tender.

Pour the remaining spice mixture over the potatoes. Garnish with mint or coriander.

Serves: 6

Pumpkin Curry *(Kaddu Ki Sabzi)*

4 tablespoons oil
pinch of asafetida
1 teaspoon turmeric powder
4 cups pumpkin, peeled and cut in small pieces
4 teaspoons coriander powder
2 teaspoons cayenne pepper
salt to taste
2 fresh chilies, seeded and chopped
1 cup water
2 teaspoons mango powder
1 teaspoon sugar
1 tablespoon dried grated coconut

Heat oil in a wok and add asafetida and turmeric. Fry 1 minute.
Add the pumpkin, coriander, cayenne, salt and chilies. Fry 2 minutes.

Add 1 cup water, cover and boil at medium heat until pumpkin is
soft.

Mash mixture with a wooden spoon. Add mango powder, sugar
and coconut.

Serves: 10-12

Spinach and Cabbage Puree *(Saag)*

This is a thick puree like mashed potatoes. We make this dish with other combinations of vegetables: turnip and spinach, carrots and spinach, cauliflower and spinach.

1 lb. fresh spinach
1 medium head of cabbage
1 cup water
2 teaspoons fresh chopped ginger root
salt to taste
½ teaspoon crushed peppercorns
2 tablespoons butter
2 teaspoons *garam masala* powder
2 teaspoons lemon juice
1 tablespoon oil
1 teaspoon cumin seeds
2 cloves garlic, chopped
2 medium onions, chopped

Wash the spinach and shred the cabbage. Boil them in water, ginger, salt and peppercorns until they are very tender, about 25 minutes in a covered saucepan, 15 minutes in a pressure cooker.

Mash the vegetables with a large wooden spoon. Add butter and boil until all the water is absorbed. Stir this mixture so that it doesn't stick to the bottom of the pan. Add *garam masala* and lemon juice. Keep mixing until the mixture is very smooth.

Heat oil in a small frying pan or saucepan and add cumin. Fry 2 minutes. Add garlic and onions. Cook 5 minutes. Pour into the vegetables and stir gently.

Serves: 8-10

Curried Spinach (*Paalak Bhaaji*)

1 lb. spinach
¾ cup water, divided
2 tablespoons oil
1 clove garlic, chopped
1 teaspoon cumin seeds
½ teaspoon turmeric powder
½ teaspoon cayenne pepper
2 teaspoons coriander powder
1 teaspoon mango powder *or*
    1 teaspoon lemon juice
salt to taste

Cook spinach in ½ cup of water in a saucepan until water evaporate. Puree the spinach.

Heat the oil in a wok and stir in the garlic and cumin seeds. Fry 2 minutes. Add everything else, except the salt, and the remaining water (¼ cup). Fry the spices for 2 minutes.

Add spinach and salt. Stir and cook until the spinach is hot.

Serves: 8

Tomato Curry (*Tamatar Ki Sabzi*)

2 tablespoons oil
1 teaspoon whole cumin seeds
1 fresh green chili, seeded and sliced
½ teaspoon turmeric powder
1 teaspoon cayenne pepper
2 teaspoons coriander powder
¼ cup water
salt to taste
2 teaspoons sugar
12 medium-sized fresh tomatoes, chopped

Heat oil in a wok. Stir in cumin seeds and green chili. Fry 2 minutes. Add the 3 powders with ¼ cup water. Add salt, sugar and the tomatoes. Simmer for 10 minutes. Remove from heat.

Serves: 6

Turnip Koftas Curry *(Shalgam Ke Koftas)*

These are vegetarian meatballs, full of protein and flavor. Instead of turnips, you can use grated zucchini or grated patty pan squash for a very different taste.

Koftas:

1 lb. turnips, white or yellow
½ cup chickpea flour
¼ cup semolina (Cream of Wheat)
3 medium onions, ground
6 cloves of garlic, ground
1 teaspoon turmeric powder
1 teaspoon cayenne pepper
2 teaspoons coriander powder
salt to taste
2 fresh green chilies, seeded and chopped
2 teaspoons chopped fresh ginger root
a few chopped coriander leaves
1 tablespoon raisins
1 cup *ghee* or oil for frying

Curry:

4 tablespoons oil
1 teaspoon cumin seeds
4 medium onions, ground
8 cloves garlic, ground
1 cup hot water
3 tomatoes, chopped *or*
    2 tablespoons tomato puree
salt to taste
1 teaspoon turmeric powder
1½ teaspoons cayenne pepper
3 teaspoons coriander powder
1 teaspoon *garam masala* powder
a few mint leaves, chopped, for garnish

For the Koftas:

Peel, slice and boil the turnips. Drain them and mash with a metal masher till they are coarsely ground. Add the next 8 ingredients. Mix well.

Make small balls and stuff each one with a little chopped chilies, ginger, coriander and raisins.

Deep fry these balls and set aside.

For the Curry:

In a wok heat the oil. Add the cumin and fry 2 minutes. Add onions and garlic and fry till onions are golden. Add hot water, tomatoes, salt and the rest of the ingredients except the *garam masala* and mint.

Cook until gravy thickens and oil separates. Just before serving add the *garam masala*. Stir. Add the koftas and stir gently. Garnish with chopped mint leaves.

Serves: 8

Mashed Zucchini Curry *(Tario Ka Bharta)*

1 lb. zucchini, peeled and ground
1 lb. medium onions, ground
2 teaspoons ground fresh garlic or garlic powder
1 teaspoon turmeric powder
1½ teaspoon cayenne pepper
3 teaspoons coriander powder
salt to taste
1 teaspoon cumin seeds
2 tablespoons ground mint leaves
1 cup tomato juice
1 tablespoon lemon juice or vinegar (any kind)
2 teaspoons *garam masala* powder
2 tablespoons *ghee*

Combine all ingredients and mix in *ghee* and salt. Cook over a low heat for 25 minutes, stirring constantly. Good with hot buttered *chappatis.*

Serves: 6-8

Zucchini Curry *(Taroi Ki Sabzi)*

6 medium zucchini
1 teaspoon turmeric powder
2 teaspoons coriander powder
1 teaspoon cumin powder
1 teaspoon cayenne pepper
1 teaspoon garlic powder
1 teaspoon ginger powder
salt to taste

Stuffing:

½ teaspoon turmeric
½ teaspoon coriander
½ teaspoon cumin
½ teaspoon cayenne pepper
½ teaspoon garlic powder
½ teaspoon ginger powder
½ teaspoon salt

Baghar:

6 tablespoons oil
1 teaspoon cumin seeds
½ teaspoon fenugreek seeds
½ teaspoon anise seed
1 teaspoon mustard seeds
½ teaspoon onion seeds
2 medium onions, sliced
½ cup hot water
1 teaspoon *garam masala* powder

Pare the zucchini and slit each zucchini lengthwise on each side but be careful not to cut all the way through.

Mix the spices for the stuffing. Fill the slits with the stuffing.

Heat oil in a wok and make *baghar* (see page 18). When the onions are golden, add the zucchini, hot water and *garam masala*. Simmer, covered, 15 minutes.

Serves: 6-8

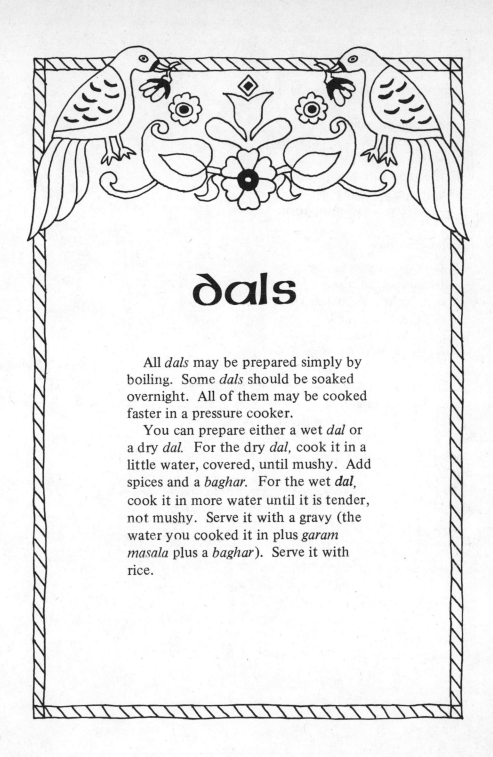

dals

All *dals* may be prepared simply by boiling. Some *dals* should be soaked overnight. All of them may be cooked faster in a pressure cooker.

You can prepare either a wet *dal* or a dry *dal.* For the dry *dal,* cook it in a little water, covered, until mushy. Add spices and a *baghar.* For the wet **dal**, cook it in more water until it is tender, not mushy. Serve it with a gravy (the water you cooked it in plus *garam masala* plus a *baghar*). Serve it with rice.

Pigeon Peas *(Toor Dal)*

This is the most popular *dal* in India.

1 cup pigeon peas
3 cups water
1 teaspoon salt
1 teaspoon turmeric powder
4 whole dried mangoes *or*
    2 tablespoons lemon juice

Baghar (see page 18):

1 tablespoon *ghee*
1 teaspoon cumin seeds
2 or 3 broken red whole chilies
4 cloves garlic, sliced
a pinch of asafetida
4-6 curry leaves, dried or fresh

Pick over the pigeon peas looking for foreign matter or discolored peas. Sometimes you will find pebbles in the peas. Wash in a sieve.

Boil the peas in water with salt, turmeric and lemon juice or mangoes (optional). Cook for 40-45 minutes or until pigeon peas are tender but still intact. (If you use a pressure cooker, it will take 15 minutes.)

Heat *ghee* and make a *baghar*. Pour over pigeon peas and stir. Adjust salt to your taste. Serve with plain boiled rice.

Serves: 6

South Indian Dal Curry *(Sambhar)*

This is a curry which is eaten every day in South India. This is a thin curry and very spicy.

Sambhar powder can be purchased in shops but the homemade powder has better flavor. See page 17 for instructions. *Sambhar* powder has a completely different taste from *garam masala*. It is yellow whereas *garam masala* is brown. Almost any vegetable can be substituted for the ones given below.

    2 cups pigeon peas
    water to cover
    1 teaspoon turmeric powder
    4 medium potatoes, raw, peeled, quartered
    2 carrots, sliced
    1 medium eggplant, sliced
    12 small onions, peeled
    12 string beans, sliced
    2 tablespoons tamarind paste
    salt to taste
    2 teaspoons *sambhar* powder

Baghar (see page 18):

    2 tablespoons oil or *ghee*
    1 teaspoon mustard seeds
    2 dried red chilies, crushed
    a few curry leaves, fresh or dried

Wash the pigeon peas. Boil them with turmeric in water until they are partially done.

Add the vegetables and cook for about ½ hour. Add the tamarind paste and salt, then the *sambhar* powder.

Make a *baghar* and pour over the curry. Stir.

Serves: 12

Curried Black Eyed Peas *(Safed Lobia)*

Black eyed peas are very popular in West Africa where I live. They are very versatile; they can be substituted for many *dals*; they can also be used in many desserts, ground fine.

Black eyed peas:

    1 cup dried black eyed peas
    3 cups water
    1 teaspoon vinegar

Sauce:

    2 tablespoons oil
    1 teaspoon cumin seeds
    1 fresh green chili, seeded and chopped
    1 medium onion, thinly sliced
    3 medium onions, ground
    1 teaspoon garlic paste or garlic powder
    1 teaspoon turmeric powder
    1 teaspoon cayenne pepper
    2 teaspoons coriander powder
    2 medium tomatoes, chopped
    salt to taste
    1 teaspoon sugar
    1 teaspoon *garam masala* powder
    1 teaspoon chopped fresh ginger root
    2 teaspoons mango powder

Garnish:

    fresh mint, chopped
    1/3 cup dried or fresh coconut, shredded (optional)
    1 lemon, quartered

For the Peas:

Boil the black eyed peas in water and vinegar till tender. Remove from heat, drain and set aside. (In a pressure cooker, it will take 20 minutes.)

For the Sauce:

In a wok heat the oil. Add cumin seeds and fry 2 minutes. Add the chili and sliced onions and fry till onions are wilted. Add the ground onions and garlic and brown well.

Add the next 3 spices plus tomatoes, salt and sugar. Stir.

Add the black eyed peas. Cook until mixture bubbles. Take off heat. Add *garam masala,* ginger and mango powder. Mix well.

Garnish.

Serves: 6

Whole Chickpeas *(Punjabi Chanas)*

This uses whole chickpeas instead of chickpea flour.

Chickpeas:

    2 cups dried chickpeas
    water to cover

Sauce:

    3 tablespoons oil
    8 medium onions, ground
    2 teaspoons ground fresh garlic
    1 teaspoon sliced ginger root
    salt to taste
    1½ teaspoons cayenne pepper
    1 teaspoon turmeric powder
    3 teaspoons coriander powder
    ½ cup hot water
    2 teaspoons *garam masala* powder
    1 teaspoon pomegranate seeds *or*
       2 tablespoons tamarind paste

Garnish:

    2 fresh green chilies, chopped
    4 potatoes, boiled, peeled and quartered
    3 medium tomatoes, chopped
    2 medium onions, sliced
    a few coriander leaves, chopped
    1 lemon, quartered

For the Chickpeas:

Soak the chickpeas overnight in water to cover. The next day, boil them until tender. If you use a pressure cooker, it will take 15 minutes. (You can use canned, drained chickpeas, or garbanzo beans, as they are sometimes called, instead.)

For the Sauce:

In a wok heat the oil. Add onions and garlic and fry till golden. Add the next 6 ingredients plus the drained chickpeas. Cook until mixture bubbles. Add *garam masala* and pomegranate seeds or tamarind paste. Stir.

For the Garnish:

Place mixture in a flat dish and decorate the top with chilies, potatoes, tomatoes, onions, coriander and lemon.

Serves: 8

Chickpea Flour Curry
(Gatta, Bela or Besan Curry)

This dish has chickpea flour noodles (either fried or boiled), in a spiced sauce.

Noodles:

2 cups chickpea flour
salt to taste
1½ teaspoon cayenne pepper
½ teaspoon carom seeds
1 tablespoon *ghee*
½ cup water for dough
2 cups salted water for boiling (½ teaspoon salt to 2 cups water)

Sauce:

½ cup yogurt
fluid left from boiling noodles
1 teaspoon turmeric powder
3 teaspoons coriander powder
2 tablespoons *ghee*
1 teaspoon cumin seeds
1 teaspoon cayenne pepper

Combination:

1 tablespoon *ghee* for frying
mint leaves, for garnish

For the Noodles:

In a large mixing bowl put the chickpea flour through a sieve. Add salt, cayenne pepper, carom seeds and *ghee*. Make a hard stiff dough by adding water. Roll the dough into long snake-like strips about 8 inches long and ½ inch thick. Boil these in salted water for about 15 minutes. When ready, remove and cut into 1 inch pieces. Set aside. Save the fluid.

For the Sauce:

Beat the yogurt with ¼ cup of the fluid. Add turmeric and coriander powder. Set aside.

Heat 2 tablespoons *ghee* in a wok. Add cumin seeds. Fry 2 minutes. Add the yogurt mixture and cayenne. Cook for 5 minutes. Add the rest of the fluid from boiling the noodles. Continue to cook till it starts to thicken. Set aside.

Combining Noodles and Curry:

Fry the strips you have previously boiled in 1 tablespoon *ghee* for a few minutes. Then add them to the curry. (The strips can be added without frying them first.) Garnish with mint.

Serves: 12

Curried Chickpeas and Patty Pan Squash
(Chana Dal and Lauki)

This dish is quite different from the one on page 104. The addition of the squash affects the taste and texture.

Vegetables:

1 cup dried chickpeas, soaked overnight
1½ cups patty pan squash, peeled and cubed
water to cover

Sauce:

2 tablespoons oil
1 teaspoon cumin seeds
4 medium onions, minced
½ cup hot water
1 teaspoon ginger powder
½ cup water
1 teaspoon turmeric powder
1 teaspoon cayenne pepper
2 teaspoons coriander powder
1 teaspoon cumin seed powder
3 medium tomatoes, chopped
salt to taste
2 teaspoons *garam masala* powder
1 teaspoon mango powder

Garnish:

mint leaves
1 fresh green chili, seeded and chopped
2 medium onions, sliced and fried

Boil chickpeas and squash in separate saucepans in water to cover. Drain. Set aside.

Heat the oil in a wok. Add cumin and fry 2 minutes. Add onions and fry till golden. Add ½ cup hot water and cook 5 minutes.

Add ginger. Mix ½ cup water with the 4 spices to form a paste. Add this and the tomatoes to the wok. Cook until oil separates.

Add salt, chickpeas and squash. Simmer 5 minutes. Take off heat. Add *garam masala* and mango powder. Garnish.

Serves: 6

Chickpea Flour Curry *(Patod or Besan Curry)*

A *Rajasthani* specialty eaten with hot buttered *rotis*. This has diamond-shaped pieces made of chickpea flour and spices in a spiced sauce.

Diamonds:

 1 cup water
 salt to taste
 1 teaspoon cayenne pepper
 1 teaspoon cumin seeds
 2 cups chickpea flour

Sauce:

 2 tablespoons *ghee* or oil
 2 or 3 dried red chilies, broken into pieces
 ½ teaspoon fenugreek seeds
 1 teaspoon mustard seeds
 3 medium onions, minced
 6 garlic cloves, chopped
 1 teaspoon turmeric powder
 1 teaspoon sliced ginger root
 ½ cup yogurt
 salt to taste
 1 green chili, seeded and chopped, for garnish
 coriander leaves, chopped, for garnish

For the Diamonds:

Bring water to a boil. Add salt, cayenne, cumin and chickpea flour. Whisk these into the water carefully. Cook until the mixture thickens.

Turn out on a greased plate and flatten with a spatula. When it cools, cut it into diamond shapes.

For the Sauce:

In a heavy saucepan heat oil or *ghee*. Add red chilies, fenugreek, mustard seeds, onions and garlic. When browned, add turmeric and sliced ginger root, yogurt and salt to taste. Cook. When it thickens a bit, about 10 minutes later, add the chickpea diamonds and simmer for 2-3 minutes. Garnish with chopped green chilies and coriander.

 Serves: 8

Steamed Bean and Vegetable Balls
(Dal Cutlets)

1 cup yellow split peas
½ cup *urad dal*
½ cup mung beans
water to cover
1 package frozen peas or equivalent in fresh peas
1 package frozen chopped spinach or a bunch of spinach
2 fresh green chilies, seeded and chopped
a few coriander leaves, chopped
3 carrots, grated
½ fresh coconut, grated
salt to taste

Baghar:

½ cup oil
½ teaspoon mustard seeds
¼ teaspoon asafetida

Soak the 3 legumes in water for 2 hours. Drain and grind coarsely. Boil the peas till tender and drain.

Thaw the spinach and mix it with green chilies, coriander leaves, grated carrots, coconut and salt.

Combine legumes, peas and spinach mixture. Set aside.

Make a *baghar*. Heat the oil in a small saucepan. Add the mustard and asafetida. Fry a few minutes. Pour over the vegetable and bean mixture.

Mix with your fingers and form small balls. Cook these in a steamer for 15 minutes.

Serves: 12

Split Mung Beans Cooked in Yogurt
(Dahi Ki Dal)

The yogurt gives this dish a delicate taste. If you like, substitute part sour cream (say, ¼ the amount) for the yogurt—this adds richness. The flavor of the spices comes out very clearly in the yogurt base.

3 tablespoons *ghee* or oil
4 medium onions, minced
8 cloves garlic, thinly sliced
1 teaspoon turmeric powder
1½ teaspoons cayenne pepper
2 teaspoons coriander powder
1¼ cup hot water, divided
1 cup split mung beans, soaked for 3 hours
1 cup yellow split peas, soaked for 3 hours
4 cups yogurt, divided
salt to taste
2 teaspoons *garam masala* powder
mint leaves, chopped, for garnish
coriander leaves, chopped, for garnish

In a wok or heavy saucepan, heat the oil. Fry the onions and garlic till golden. Add the 3 powdered spices plus ¼ cup of hot water and cook till it bubbles.

Drain the split mung beans and yellow split peas. Add them to the wok along with 2 cups yogurt. Cook 10 minutes at medium heat. Add salt and remaining cup of hot water. Cook again.

When the legumes are tender, add salt and remaining yogurt (2 cups) and simmer 10 minutes more.

Remove from heat. Add *garam masala* powder, stir and garnish.

Serves: 6

Pink Lentil Curry *(Masoor Dal)*

This is the quickest *dal* to cook—it takes only 20 minutes without using a pressure cooker. The pink color of the lentils becomes pale yellow once it is cooked. The flavor is more subtle than the green lentils.

1 cup pink lentils
3 cups water
1 teaspoon turmeric powder
1 teaspoon salt
1 tablespoon lemon juice
1 teaspoon *garam masala* powder

Baghar:

1 tablespoon oil or *ghee*
1 teaspoon cumin seeds
1 teaspoon cayenne pepper
1 teaspoon coriander powder

Garnish:

2 slices onion, fried till golden in oil
a few chopped fresh coriander or mint leaves

Carefully pick over the lentils, discarding discolored ones or any foreign matter. Wash in a sieve under running water. In a heavy saucepan boil the lentils in water with turmeric. When cooked, turn off heat; add salt, lemon juice and *garam masala.*

Heat *ghee;* add cumin seeds. Fry 2 minutes. Turn off heat. Add cayenne and coriander. Stir and pour over the cooked lentils. Mix well. Garnish.

Serves: 6

Urad Dal *(Maah Ki Dal)*

This is a popular *punjabi* dish which is eaten by rich and poor with hot buttered *chappatis.*

1 cup *urad dal*
4 cups water
1 teaspoon *ghee*
1 teaspoon turmeric powder
2 whole red chilies, broken
1 teaspoon chopped ginger root
6 cloves garlic, sliced
1 teaspoon *garam masala* powder
1 tablespoon lemon juice
salt to taste

Baghar:

1 tablespoon *ghee*
1 teaspoon cumin seeds
1 teaspoon cayenne pepper
1 teaspoon coriander powder
½ fresh green chili, seeded and chopped

Carefully pick over the *urad dal* and discard any discolored ones or foreign matter. Wash in sieve under running cold water.

Place in a heavy saucepan and boil in water, with *ghee,* turmeric, red chili, ginger and garlic. Cook approximately 40 minutes or until done. (Pressure cooker takes about 15 minutes.) Take off heat. Add *garam masala* powder, lemon juice and salt. Stir.

Make a *baghar.* Heat *ghee* in a small saucepan and fry cumin seeds till they change color slightly. Turn off heat and add cayenne, coriander and green chili. If you continued cooking the mixture, the cayenne pepper would burn. Pour the *baghar* over the *urad dal* and mix well.

Serves: 6

Split Mung Bean Kofta
(Moong Ki Dal Ka Kofta)

This is a very exotic dish, rich with saffron and pistachios.

Kofta:

    2 cups split mung beans
    water to cover
    2 medium onions, finely chopped
    8 cloves garlic, ground *or*
        1 teaspoon garlic powder
    1 teaspoon fresh ginger *or*
        1 teaspoon ginger powder
    1 teaspoon cayenne pepper
    1 teaspoon *garam masala* powder
    2 teaspoons coriander powder
    salt to taste
    a few chopped coriander leaves
    4 tablespoons *ghee*
    1 cup water
    1 cup *ghee* or oil for frying

Curry:

    4 tablespoons *ghee* or oil
    6 cloves
    8 medium onions, ground
    ½ cup hot water
    6 cloves garlic, ground
    1 teaspoon ground ginger root
    2 tablespoons ground poppy seeds
    1 teaspoon turmeric powder
    1½ teaspoons cayenne pepper
    3 teaspoons coriander powder
    1 cup yogurt
    salt to taste
    1 teaspoon *garam masala* powder
    pinch of saffron
    12 pistachios, chopped

Garnish:

2 onions, sliced and fried
coriander or mint leaves, chopped
2 leaves of edible silver paper

For the Koftas:

Soak the split mung beans in water 2 hours. Drain and grind very fine in blender. Put in a saucepan.

Add onions, garlic, the spices, salt, coriander leaves, *ghee* and water. Cook 5-10 minutes.

Put in a bowl and knead. Set aside for ½ hour and then make small balls.

Deep-fry these in hot *ghee* or oil. Set aside.

For the Curry:

In a saucepan, heat oil and fry cloves till they change color a bit. Add ground onions and fry a deep brown.

Add hot water plus garlic, ginger and poppy seeds (ground in a blender). Cook for 5 minutes. Add turmeric, cayenne and coriander, yogurt and salt. Simmer 15 minutes.

Remove from heat. Add *garam masala* , saffron and nuts. Let the curry cool down a bit and then add the koftas, gently. The koftas should not sit in the curry too long, they will disintegrate. Nor should the curry be boiling hot when the koftas are added.

Garnish with fried onions and chopped mint or coriander leaves. Decorate with edible silver paper.

Serves: 8-10

Curried Green Split Peas *(Matar Ki Dal)*

You can buy the *badis* (made of *dal* paste and curry and dried in the sun) used in this dish or you can make them (see page 18). It will be much easier to buy them and the difference in taste is inconsequential.

2 cups green split peas
2 cups pumpkin, peeled and cubed
water to cover
4 tablespoons oil
¼ lb. *badis*
3 medium onions, ground
1 teaspoon garlic powder *or* garlic paste
1 teaspoon ginger paste or powder
1 teaspoon ground cumin seeds
1 teaspoon turmeric powder
1 teaspoon cayenne pepper
2 teaspoons coriander powder
1 teaspoon ground black pepper
1½ cups hot water, divided
salt to taste
4 dried mangoes

Baghar:

1 tablespoon oil
1 teaspoon *garam masala,* whole
2 cloves garlic, sliced
1 fresh green chili, seeded and chopped

Boil the split peas in water to cover till done. Drain and set aside. Boil the pumpkin in water to cover till done. Drain and set aside. In a wok, heat oil and fry *badis*. Remove and set aside.

In the same wok, fry onions, garlic and all the spices. Pour in a half cup of hot water so that the spices will not burn. Cook 5 minutes.

Add the green split peas, pumpkin and 1 more cup of hot water. Bring to a boil.

Add salt, fried *badis* and mangoes. Simmer, covered, for 30 minutes over medium heat. Stir occasionally.

Make a *baghar* (see page 18), pour over the curry and stir.

Serves: 12

Poppadam Curry *(Papad Ka Saag)*

6 poppadams
2 tablespoons *ghee* or oil
1 teaspoon cumin seeds
4 medium onions, minced
6 garlic cloves, ground
½ cup beaten yogurt
2 teaspoons cayenne pepper
1 teaspoon turmeric powder
4 teaspoons coriander powder
salt to taste

Roast poppadams over a gas flame. Break each one into 6-8 pieces. Set aside.

In a heavy skillet or wok, heat *ghee* or oil. Add cumin seeds. Fry 1 minute.

Add onions and garlic. Fry until onions are golden. Add the yogurt, the spices and salt. Simmer for about 15 minutes. Add the broken poppadams and simmer for 5 minutes.

Serves: 8-10

egg
dishes

Slowly, as eggs become more available in India, they are becoming more popular. Many vegetarian Hindus are beginning to eat eggs, formerly forbidden to them.

Since eggs are a comparatively new addition to Indian cooking, some of these recipes are my own adaptations of Western recipes, with the addition of Indian spices.

Eggs in Yogurt *(Dahi Ke Ande)*

2 cups yogurt
½ teaspoon cayenne pepper
¼ teaspoon turmeric powder
1 teaspoon cumin powder
salt to taste
6 hard-cooked eggs

Baghar (see page 18):

1 tablespoon oil
1 teaspoon cumin seeds
1 fresh green chili, seeded and chopped

Beat the yogurt with a fork. Blend in the spices and salt.

Peel the eggs and cut in half lengthwise. Place in a serving dish and pour seasoned yogurt over the eggs.

Make a *baghar* of oil, cumin and chili. Pour over the eggs and yogurt.

Serves: 12

Egg and Potato Curry *(Anda and Aloo Curry)*

If you use yogurt instead of water, the taste will be creamier.

4 tablespoons oil
1 teaspoon cumin seeds
4 medium onions, grated
4 cloves garlic, crushed
½ cup hot water
4 fresh tomatoes, chopped *or*
    1 tablespoon tomato puree
1 teaspoon turmeric powder
1 teaspoon cayenne pepper
2 teaspoons coriander powder
salt to taste
1 cup yogurt *or*
    1 cup hot water
6 hard-cooked eggs, peeled and chopped
6 boiled potatoes, peeled and quartered
1 teaspoon *garam masala* powder
juice of 1 lemon
fresh mint leaves, chopped, for garnish

Heat oil in a wok or saucepan. Add cumin seeds and fry 1 minute. Add the onions and garlic and fry till golden.

Add ½ cup hot water, tomatoes, spices and salt. Simmer, covered, for 5 minutes.

Add 1 cup of yogurt or hot water, then the eggs and potatoes. Simmer, covered, for 5 minutes.

Turn off the heat. Add *garam masala* and lemon juice. Stir. Garnish with mint leaves.

Serves: 12

Omelette Curry

Omelettes:

8 eggs, beaten
2 onions, finely chopped
1 fresh green chili, seeded and finely chopped
salt to taste
1 tablespoon *ghee* for frying

Curry:

4 tablespoons oil
1 teaspoon cumin
4 onions, grated
2 tablespoons tomato puree
2 teaspoons curry powder
1 cup hot water
salt to taste
1 teaspoon *garam masala* powder
mint leaves, chopped, for garnish

Make four omelettes and cut into strips. Set aside.

Heat oil in a saucepan. Add cumin and onions and fry well. Add the tomato puree and curry powder, then hot water. Let simmer, covered, for 10 minutes. Add salt and *garam masala.*

Remove from heat. Add the omelette strips carefully so that they do not break. Pour into a serving dish and garnish with mint.

Serves: 6-8

Eggless Omelette

½ cup water, approximately
1 medium onion, chopped
2 green chilies, seeded and chopped
a few chopped coriander or mint leaves
¼ teaspoon cayenne pepper
1 cup rice flour
½ cup chickpea flour

 salt to taste
2 teaspoons *ghee*

Mix all the ingredients except the *ghee* into a thick batter.

Grease a teflon or non-stick pan with *ghee* or oil. Pour in a little batter and cover the pan. When cooked on one side, flip it over and cook on the other side. Repeat until all the batter is used.

Serve hot with ketchup.

Serves: 6

Baked Eggs in Tomato Shells

6 large ripe tomatoes
salt to sprinkle on tomatoes
3 teaspoons of butter
6 eggs
salt to taste
¼ teaspoon black pepper
¼ teaspoon cayenne pepper
3 tablespoons grated cheddar cheese
3 tablespoons chopped coriander leaves *or*
    mint leaves, for garnish

Cut a thin slice from the top of each tomato. Scoop out the pulp. Salt the tomatoes lightly and turn upside down to drain for about 10 minutes. Arrange the tomatoes right-side up in a well-buttered baking dish and place a half teaspoon of butter in each tomato. Bake for 5 minutes at 350 degrees.

Break one egg into each tomato shell. Bake until the egg white has set, about 10 minutes. Mix together the salt, pepper, cayenne pepper and grated cheese. Sprinkle a little of this mixture over the top of each egg. Place under the broiler until the cheese melts.

Garnish with coriander or mint leaves.

Serves: 6

Stuffed Tomatoes with Eggs

6 large tomatoes
6 beaten eggs
2 onions, chopped
1 fresh green chili, seeded and chopped
salt to taste
1 teaspoon *garam masala*
a few chopped fresh coriander leaves
1 teaspoon butter
¼ cup oil for frying

Sealing Paste:

2 tablespoons whole wheat flour
1 tablespoon water

Wash tomatoes. Cut off tops and scoop out pulp. Save the pulp for soup or any other dish.

Beat the eggs and add onion, chili and seasonings. Melt 1 teaspoon butter in skillet and scramble the eggs.

Fill the tomatoes with the eggs. Make a paste of flour and water. Seal the tops of the tomatoes.

Fry the tomatoes in ¼ cup hot oil. Turn these so that they are completely cooked. It will take about 6 minutes.

When you serve these, remove the paste lids first.

Serves: 6

Eggs with Rice *(Anda Pullao)*

2 cups of raw rice
8 hard-cooked eggs, shelled
4 tablespoons oil or *ghee*
2 bay leaves
1 teaspoon whole *garam masala*
2 medium onions, ground
4 cloves garlic, ground
1 teaspoon turmeric powder
1 teaspoon red cayenne pepper
2 teaspoons coriander powder
salt to taste
4 cups water
1 tablespoon raisins
2 medium onions, sliced and fried, for garnish

Soak the rice for 20 minutes.

Puncture each egg with an ice pick, or tip of a sharp knife. This will permit the curry flavors to penetrate the eggs. Fry the eggs in oil until light brown. Remove.

In the same skillet fry bay leaves and *garam masala*. Fry 2 minutes. Add the onions and garlic and fry till they are golden.

Add the 3 powdered spices, salt and 4 cups of water. Also add the eggs and raisins.

Cook, covered, over low heat until rice is tender, about 20 minutes. Garnish with fried onions.

Serves: 8

Rice dishes

Rice, the favorite grain of the Moguls, is a staple in Southern India and along the Northeastern belt. Rice may be cooked in many ways: boiled in water or in coconut milk, steamed, or curried. Please note white rice only is used in Indian cooking.

There are various ways to serve rice. It can be placed in a mound on a flat plate; spooned into a greased jello mold or small bowl, pressed flat, unmolded, on a serving plate and garnished with parsley or mint leaves; served in small bowls and garnished with omelette strips; or placed in a fancy, greased ring mold, unmolded and filled with curry.

Boiled Rice with Cumin *(Chawal)*

2 cups raw long-grained rice
4 cups water
1 teaspoon salt
1 teaspoon butter or *ghee* (optional)

Baghar (see page 18):

1 tablespoon *ghee*
1 teaspoon cumin seeds

Wash the rice thoroughly until the water is absolutely clear. Drain. Combine rice, water and salt in a heavy saucepan and cook, uncovered, over medium-high heat for 10 minutes. Place the lid on top and turn off the heat. Let the rice sit on the stove for 10-15 minutes before taking off the lid. Put *ghee* around the inside edges of the pan. This enhances the taste and appearance.

The rice can be seasoned with a *baghar*. Pour it over the top of the rice. Stir and serve.

Serves: 6

Vegetables and Rice *(Sabzi Biryani)*

3 cups raw long-grain rice
6 cups water

4 tablespoons oil
1 teaspoon cumin seeds
2 medium onions, thinly sliced
½ lb. cauliflower, chopped
½ lb. potatoes, peeled and cubed
¼ lb. green peas
¼ lb. green beans, chopped
1 teaspoon turmeric powder
salt to taste
3 tablespoons *garam masala* powder
1 cup yogurt

1 cup *ghee*
juice of 4 lemons
¼ teaspoon saffron, soaked in 2 teaspoons warm milk
1 cup chopped mint leaves
1 cup chopped coriander leaves

Cook the rice with water in a covered saucepan for 15-20 minutes.
Set aside.

In a wok, heat the oil and add cumin seeds. Fry 2 minutes. Stir
and add the sliced onions. Fry till they are golden.

Add all the vegetables and fry them for 2 minutes. Cover and
simmer for 5 minutes more. Add turmeric, salt and *garam masala.*

Taste one of the vegetables. If it is not sufficiently cooked, add
½ cup hot water, cover and cook a few minutes more.

Add the yogurt and stir gently.

Grease a heavy pan or flame-proof casserole. Put a layer of vegetables, a layer of rice, a tablespoon of warm *ghee,* a tablespoon of
lemon juice, some saffron-flavored milk and lots of chopped mint
and coriander leaves.

Repeat layering until all ingredients are used up. Cover the pan
and simmer on very low heat 20 minutes.

Serves: 8-10

Fried Rice *(Taheri)*

4 cups rice
water to cover

8 tablespoons oil
10 medium potatoes, peeled and halved
½ cauliflower, chopped
2 bay leaves
4 cardamom seeds
4 cloves
pinch of asafetida
½ cup split mung beans
½ cup green peas
1 teaspoon turmeric powder
salt to taste
2 teaspoons raisins
1 cup yogurt
9 cups water

Soak the rice for 20 minutes. Drain. Set aside.

In a wok, heat the oil and fry the potatoes and cauliflower. When browned, remove them and set aside.

In the same wok put bay leaves, cardamom, cloves and asafetida. Fry 2 minutes. Add the drained rice, mung beans, peas, turmeric and salt. Stir and fry until moisture goes from the rice and the rice starts to turn color.

Add raisins, yogurt and water. Cook, covered, until all the water is absorbed, about 20 minutes. Turn off heat and keep covered for about 10 minutes.

Serves: 8

Lemon Rice *(Neebu Chawal)*

This is a very popular form of rice eaten in Southern India. It tastes good eaten either warm or cold. It keeps well (2-3 days without refrigeration) and therefore is useful to take on a picnic or on journeys.

3 cups rice
6 cups water

3 tablespoons oil
1 teaspoon mustard seeds
1 teaspoon yellow split peas
2 fresh green chilies, seeded and chopped
2 tablespoons turmeric powder
2 tablespoons peanuts or cashews, roasted
4 tablespoons lemon juice
a few curry leaves, dried or fresh
salt to taste

Boil the rice in water 3-4 hours before using it in this recipe. (You can use leftover rice instead, if you wish.) When rice is cold, break it apart with your fingers.

Heat oil in a saucepan and add mustard seeds. Fry till they pop. Add yellow split peas and chilies. Fry 2 minutes more. Add turmeric, peanuts, lemon juice and curry leaves. Cook 5 minutes. Add the salt.

Remove from heat and gradually stir in the boiled rice. Cover to keep flavors sealed in. Remove cover just before serving.

Serves: 6-8

Tamarind Rice *(Imli Chawal)*

The tamarind helps preserve this rice—it will keep 3 days or so without refrigeration.

3 cups rice
6 cups water

salt to taste
½ cup tamarind juice (see page 15)
3 dried red chilies, crushed

Baghar (see page 18):

2 tablespoons oil
1 teaspoon mustard seeds
1 teaspoon *urad dal*
1 fresh chili, seeded and chopped

Cook rice in water for 20 minutes in a covered saucepan. Cool it for 30 minutes.

Add the salt, tamarind juice and red chilies.

Make a *baghar* of oil, mustard seeds, *urad dal* and green chili. Add it to the spiced rice and stir. Heat the rice through for 5 minutes and stir.

Serves: 6-8

Mango Rice (Aam Chawal)

3 cups rice
6 cups water

1 teaspoon turmeric powder
3 dried red chilies, crushed
salt to taste
1 green mango, sliced

3 tablespoons oil
a pinch of asafetida
1 teaspoon mustard seeds
1 teaspoon yellow split peas
a few curry leaves, dried or fresh

Cook the rice in water in a covered saucepan 15-20 minutes until done.

Add the turmeric, red chilies, salt and mango and mix thoroughly. Set aside.

In a saucepan, heat oil and add asafetida, mustard seeds, yellow split peas and curry leaves. Fry several minutes.

Add the rice. Stir and cook for 5-10 minutes until mango is blended with the rice.

Serves: 6

Yogurt Rice *(Dahi Chawal)*

2 cups yogurt
4 cups boiled rice
salt to taste
2 tablespoons oil
1 teaspoon mustard seeds
1 teaspoon *urad dal*
1 teaspoon yellow split peas
1 fresh green chili, seeded and chopped

Mix the yogurt with the rice and salt. Heat oil; add mustard seeds, *urad dal,* yellow split peas, and green chili. Fry 2 minutes then add the rice mixture. Turn off the heat immediately. Cool thoroughly. This is served cold.

Serves: 8

Tomato Rice *(Tamatar Chawal)*

This dish brings back nostalgic memories as it was served on Saturday mornings at the M.G.D. School in Jaipur.

2 cups rice
4 cups water

2 tablespoons oil
1 teaspoon sesame seeds
4 medium tomatoes, chopped
1 fresh green chili, seeded and chopped
1 teaspoon cayenne pepper
salt to taste

Cook the rice in water in a covered saucepan for 15-20 minutes. Set aside when done.

In a skillet, heat the oil and add the sesame seeds. Fry 2 minutes. Add the tomatoes, chili, cayenne, salt and cooked rice. Fry until tomatoes are soft.

Serves: 6

Green Rice *(Hara Chawal)*

4 tablespoons oil
1 teaspoon cumin seeds
½ teaspoon peppercorns
4 whole cloves
2 bay leaves
2 medium onions, sliced
3 fresh green chilies, seeded and ground
1 cup of ground mint or coriander leaves *or*
    1 cup finely chopped spinach
salt to taste
3 cups rice
6 cups water

Heat oil and put in cumin seeds, peppercorns, cloves and bay leaves. Fry 2 minutes. Add the onions; stir and fry until they are golden brown. Then add the ground green chilies, mint, salt and rice. Fry for 5-10 minutes. Then add the water. Cover and cook until the water is absorbed. Turn off the heat. Keep warm until ready to serve.

Serves: 6-8

Coconut Rice

The coconut milk adds a fresh, sweet taste to this dish.

2 coconuts, cracked
4 cups hot water

2 tablespoons oil or *ghee*
2 teaspoons cumin seeds
2 fresh green chilies, seeded and chopped
2 cups rice, soaked 20 minutes and drained
salt to taste
1 teaspoon turmeric powder

Peel the coconuts and cut in small pieces (see page 18). Grind in a blender with hot water. Strain. There should be 4 cups. If not, add a little water. Set aside.

Heat the oil and add cumin and chilies. Fry 2-3 minutes. Add the drained rice, salt, turmeric and coconut milk.

Cook over low heat until all the liquid is absorbed. Turn off heat. Let sit, covered, on stove 10-15 minutes before serving.

Serves: 4-6

Rice and Lentil Kedgeree *(Khichri)*

2 tablespoons oil
1 teaspoon cumin seeds
4 cloves, ground
½ cup mung beans
3 cups rice
1 teaspoon turmeric powder
salt to taste
7 cups water
4 teaspoons *ghee*

Heat oil. Add cumin and cloves and fry 2 minutes. Add the beans, rice, turmeric, salt and water. Let it cook, covered, over medium heat until the rice is done. It should be soft, like scrambled eggs. Serve on four individual plates. Make a well in the center of the kedgeree and put 1 teaspoon of the *ghee* there. Serve hot.

Serves: 4

Rice with Green Peas *(Matar Pullao)*

This is the most popular kind of rice served at parties in Indian homes. It is also the most popular rice dish served in Indian restaurants.

4 tablespoons oil
1 teaspoon cumin seeds
4 cloves
1 stick cinnamon
2 tablespoons raisins
1 medium onion, sliced
½ cup green peas
2 cups long-grained rice, soaked for 20 minutes and drained
salt to taste
2 fresh green chilies, seeded and sliced
4½ cups water
2 onions, sliced and fried, for garnish

In a large heavy saucepan heat oil and add cumin seeds, cloves, cinnamon and raisins. Fry 2 minutes. Add sliced onion and fry 2 minutes.

Add peas, drained rice, salt and chilies. Cook until onions are soft. Then add 4½ cups water, cover and cook for 20 minutes.

Turn off heat and keep rice covered until ready to serve.

Garnish with fried onions.

Serves: 4-6

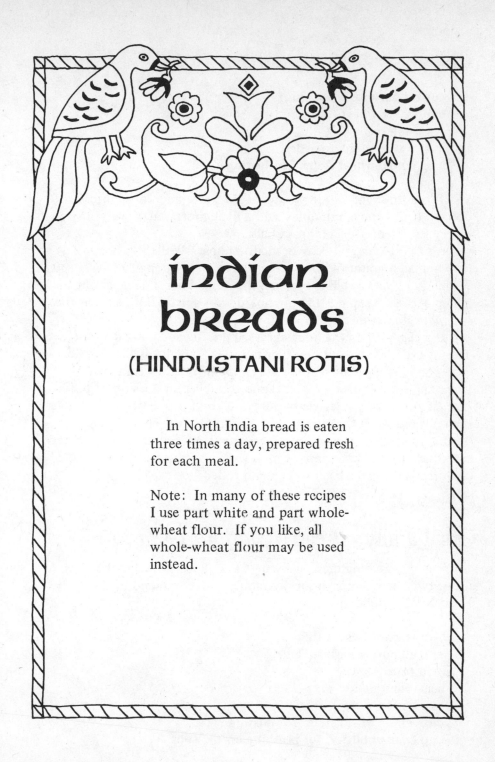

indian breads

(HINDUSTANI ROTIS)

In North India bread is eaten three times a day, prepared fresh for each meal.

Note: In many of these recipes I use part white and part whole-wheat flour. If you like, all whole-wheat flour may be used instead.

Indian Bread *(Chappatis or Roti)*

    1 cup all-purpose white flour
    1 cup whole-wheat flour
    1 teaspoon salt
    ½ cup water, more if needed
    ½ cup whole-wheat flour, for dusting

Sift the flour and salt in a bowl. Add water and knead into a stiff dough. If the dough crumbles, add a little more water until the dough can be gathered into a compact ball.

Heat a cast-iron griddle over medium heat. While it is heating up, take a small amount of dough, the size of a ping pong ball and flatten it slightly. Using a rolling pin, roll the dough into a circle about 5 inches across. Keep dusting the board with a little flour so that the *chappatis* don't stick.

Put a *chappati* on the hot ungreased griddle and cook a minute. Turn it over. Cook it for another minute. Take it off the griddle.

If you have a gas stove, take the *chappati* firmly with a pair of tongs and roast it over a direct flame about 1 minute, until it puffs out. If you have an electric stove, use a cross-grained wire mesh over the coils and roast the *chappati* on it until it puffs out.

Chappatis are best eaten hot from the stove, but they are also good served at room temperature. Children like them spread with a layer of butter and then a layer of jam and rolled.

Yields: 12

Our Family's Bread *(Khatipura Ki Roti)*

I remember eating these every day as a child. Now I make them about two times a month for my family. I recommend these highly. They are very delicious.

    2½ cups whole-wheat flour
    ¾ cup all-purpose white flour
    salt to taste
    2 teaspoons melted *ghee*
    ½ cup water
    ½ cup whole-wheat flour, for dusting
    ½ cup *ghee* or butter, for brushing on the tops

Sift the flour and salt together in a bowl. Add *ghee* and rub the flour and *ghee* together with your fingertips until the mixture looks like coarse meal. Add water and knead into a compact ball.

Take a small amount of dough, the size of a ping pong ball and roll out, on a lightly floured surface, a circle about 6 inches in diameter.

Brush it with *ghee* and sprinkle some flour over it. Fold it in half. Brush it once more with *ghee* and sprinkle flour over it. Fold it a second time to form a triangle. Roll the triangle to make it bigger.

Heat an ungreased cast-iron griddle. Roast the *roti* on one side about 1 minute, pressing on several spots with a folded napkin so that each layer of the *roti* will cook. Repeat on the other side for 1 minute, again pressing with the folded napkin. The *roti* will puff up.

Take the *roti* off the griddle. Tap it several times lightly on a board to let the air escape. Prick one side of the *roti* with the end of a spoon and then brush with *ghee*. The *ghee* will penetrate through the layers of the *roti*. Brush *ghee* on the other side of the *roti*.

These can be stored 2 days in a cloth napkin or frozen. They are at their best freshly made and fragrant with the aroma of wheat and *ghee*.

Yields: 12

Paranthas

The ingredients are the same as for *chappatis,* but rolling out the dough is a little different.

Take a small amount of dough and form it into a ball. Roll it out on a lightly floured board to a circle about 6 inches across. Spread a teaspoon of *ghee* or oil on the *parantha*. Fold the dough in half and then fold it in half again.

Roll the triangle until it is again about 6 inches across. Roast it 1 minute on a heated cast-iron griddle. Turn it over after 1 minute and cook on the other side.

Apply oil or *ghee* on both sides. Roast for another minute on both sides until crisp. Drain on paper towels. Keep them stacked inside a *chappati* box or wrapped in aluminum foil. These taste best hot, but they are fine at room temperature too.

Yields: 12

Potato-Filled Bread *(Aloo Paranthas)*

Filling:

6 medium potatoes, boiled, peeled and mashed
1 fresh green chili, seeded and chopped
1 teaspoon salt
1 teaspoon cumin seeds
1 teaspoon *garam masala* powder
½ teaspoon cayenne pepper
2 teaspoons mango powder
1 medium onion, minced

Dough:

2 cups flour
1 teaspoon salt
2 tablespoons oil
½ cup water
½ cup oil for frying

Combine the ingredients for the filling. Be careful to blend well. Set aside.

Make the dough, as in *paranthas* (see preceding page). Divide the dough into 12 balls. Flatten these with the palm of your hand and roll them out with a rolling pin on a floured board, one at a time, forming circles 6 inches across.

Place 1 tablespoon of the filling in the center of each circle. Bring the outside ring of dough up and over the filling and pinch the dough over the filling so that it is completely covered.

Turn the dough over and flatten it with the palm of your hand. Roll it out again to a circle 6 inches across.

Roast the *paranthas* on both sides in a little oil on a hot griddle.

Yields: 12

Fried Horseradish Bread *(Muli Ka Parantha)*

We eat this in India during the winter months when horseradish is available.

4 cups grated horseradish
½ cup water to boil the horseradish
1 teaspoon salt
1 teaspoon cayenne pepper
1 medium onion, chopped
1 teaspoon mango powder
6 cloves garlic, ground
1 teaspoon *garam masala* powder
1 teaspoon roasted, ground cumin seeds
a few coriander leaves, chopped
2 cups whole-wheat flour
½ cup water, approximately, for the dough
½ cup oil for frying

Boil the horseradish in ½ cup of water. Drain. Mix all the seasonings with the boiled horseradish. Add flour and ½ cup water to make a stiff dough.

Roll out on a floured board to a circle 6 inches wide.

Heat a cast-iron griddle. Put a tablespoon of oil on the griddle and brush it over the surface of the griddle. Put the *parantha* on the hot griddle, adding a little more oil around the edges, if necessary. Cook until nicely browned. Repeat on the other side.

Yields: 10-12

Egg Bread *(Egg or Omelette Paranthas)*

Egg Batter:

  4 eggs, beaten
  1 teaspoon cumin seeds
  1 medium onion, minced
  1 fresh green chili, seeded and chopped
  salt to taste
  1 teaspoon cayenne pepper

Dough:

  2 cups whole wheat flour
  1 teaspoon salt
  ½ cup water
  ½ cup oil for frying

Combine all the ingredients for the batter. Set aside.

Combine the flour, salt and water to make a stiff dough. Divide dough into 12-14 equal balls. Flatten balls with the palm of your hand and roll out each one into a 5 inch circle.

Fry on a hot griddle with a little oil. Pour a spoonful of the batter over the *parantha*. When nicely browned, turn it over and pour another spoonful of batter and a little more oil around the edges. Turn it over once more and brush the surface with oil. Remove. Repeat for the other *paranthas*.

  Yields: 12-14

Green Coriander Bread *(Hara Dhaniya Ka)*

2 cups whole wheat flour
salt to taste
1 teaspoon cumin seeds
1 teaspoon cayenne pepper
1 cup ground coriander leaves *or* spinach leaves
½ cup water, approximately
½ cup oil for frying

Combine all the ingredients (except the oil for frying) into a stiff dough. Roll into circles 6 inches across. Fry like plain *paranthas* (see page 141).

Yields: 10-12

Spicy Bread *(Masala Roti)*

1 cup chickpea flour
2 cups whole wheat flour
1 medium onion, finely chopped
1 fresh green chili, seeded and chopped
1 teaspoon cumin powder
salt to taste
1 teaspoon cayenne pepper
¾ cup of water, approximately
2 tablespoons *ghee*

Mix the ingredients, except the *ghee*, into a stiff dough. Divide into 12-16 equal balls.

Roll out to circles 6 inches wide. Roast on both sides on an ungreased heated griddle.

After each one is roasted, put about ½ teaspoon *ghee* on each and stack. Wrap the stack in aluminum foil to keep hot.

Yields: 12-16

Deep-Fried Bread *(Puris)*

Puris are only made on special occasions. They stay fresh for 2-3 days.

2 cups whole wheat flour
1 teaspoon salt
2 tablespoons oil
½ cup water or more
2 cups oil for frying

Sift the flour and add salt, oil and water and knead with your hands until a stiff dough is formed. Divide into 16 balls.

Roll out each ball to a 4 inch circle on a greased board.

Heat 2 cups of oil in a wok and fry each *puri*. When one side is browned, press it with a flat spoon so that it puffs up and turns over. Take it out within a half a minute. Drain on a paper towel.

Yields: 16

Stuffed Fried Bread *(Stuffed Puris)*

Filling:

½ cup *urad dal*
2 tablespoons oil
1 teaspoon cumin seeds
1 teaspoon salt
1 teaspoon turmeric powder
1 teaspoon cayenne pepper
¼ cup water

Dough:

2 cups whole wheat flour
1 teaspoon salt
2 tablespoons oil
½ cup water
2 cups oil for frying

For the Filling:

Soak *urad dal* overnight in water to cover. Drain. Heat oil and
add *urad dal,* cumin seeds, salt and spices. Fry for 2-3 minutes. Add
¼ cup water and simmer till *urad dal* is tender.

For the Dough:

Sift flour and salt. Add the oil and water. Blend well. Then
divide into 16 balls and roll out on a greased board to circles 4 inches
in diameter.

Put a tablespoonful of filling on each circle. Draw up the edges of
the circle and seal the filling inside. Flatten by gently rolling them on
a greased board.

Heat oil in a wok and deep-fry one or two at a time. Drain on a
paper towel. These will keep 3-4 days.

Yields: 16

Fried Bread *(Bhatura)*

2 cups all-purpose white flour
½ teaspoon salt
1 teaspoon baking soda
1 egg
½ cup yogurt
1 teaspoon sugar
2 teaspoons *ghee* or vegetable oil
½ cup water
2 cups oil for frying

In a bowl, combine the flour, salt and soda. Add egg, yogurt, sugar, *ghee* and water to make a stiff dough. Knead well. Cover with a dampened dishtowel and set aside in a warm place for at least 4 hours, so that dough can rise.

Divide the dough into 8 equal balls. Roll each ball of dough into rounds about 4 inches in diameter, one-half inch thick. Deep-fry them one at a time and drain on a paper towel.

Excellent with chickpea curry.

Yields: 8

Barbecued Bread *(Tandoori Roti)*

2 cups whole-wheat flour
1 teaspoon salt
½ cup water
1 tablespoon *ghee,* approximately, for brushing

In a deep bowl, combine flour, salt and water to make a stiff dough. Divide the dough into 10 balls and roll each into a thick circle about 6 inches in diameter and ½ inch thick. Dampen with water on one side and put on a *tandoor* or place them on a baking sheet and bake in an oven at 350 degrees for 10 minutes. Stack when all are baked. Then grease one side of each bread with *ghee* and place under a broiler for 3 minutes. Serve hot.

Yields: 10

Deep-Fried Potato Bread *(Kulcha)*

2 cups all-purpose white flour
1 teaspoon salt
1 teaspoon sugar
1 cup potatoes, peeled, boiled and mashed
1 teaspoon baking powder
1 egg
1 cup yogurt
1 tablespoon *ghee* or oil
a little water to knead
2 cups oil for frying

Sift the flour and add salt, sugar, potatoes, baking powder, egg, yogurt and *ghee*. Mix together and make into a dough with a little water. Cover and keep in a warm place for 2 hours so that it can rise. Divide dough into 8 balls and roll out into 8 circles about 4 inches in diameter and ½ inch thick. Deep-fry in hot oil in a wok.

Yields: 8

Bread Rolls *(Batis Rajasthani)*

2 cups whole wheat flour
1 teaspoon salt
1 cup *ghee* divided
1 cup yogurt or milk
sufficient water to knead

Sift the flour and salt. Add ½ cup melted *ghee* and yogurt. Adding water gradually make a stiff dough.

Divide dough into 12 equal balls. Bake in a 350 degree oven for 30 minutes. Remove them from oven.

Make a cross with a sharp knife on the top of the balls. Fry all the balls in a big wok with ½ cup of *ghee* until they are golden brown in color. If you wish to add more *ghee* to the wok, do so.

These can be stuffed with curried mashed potatoes before baking.

Yields: 12

Raised Bread *(Naan)*

This is very popular on the Northwestern border of India. They are traditionally baked in a *tandoor,* a clay oven buried in the ground. *Tandoors* are now available which can be placed on top of any gas stove. *Naans* may be also baked on a cookie sheet in a hot oven.

2 cups white flour
1 teaspoon salt
1 teaspoon sugar
½ cup milk
2 tablespoons *ghee*
½ cup yogurt
1 egg
1 teaspoon baking soda
1 teaspoon baking powder
1 tablespoon *ghee,* for brushing on top of the *naan*
1 tablespoon onion seeds

In a deep bowl combine the flour, salt and sugar. Add milk, *ghee,* yogurt, egg, baking soda and powder. Mix into a soft dough.

Sprinkle a little flour over the dough. Cover with a dampened dishcloth and let rest in a warm place 4 hours so that it can rise. The dough will be elastic. Take a small ball of it and pull it with your hands into the shape of a footprint. Brush a little *ghee* on one side and a few onion seeds. Apply water with your hand on the other side. Stick the wet side of the *naan* on a cookie sheet and bake in a 400 degree oven 5-10 minutes. You can brush with more *ghee* if you like.

For quicker results, you can cook the naan on a heated iron griddle on the stove . Cook one side only. Finish the naan under the broiler for a minute, after brushing it with ghee and onion seeds.

Yields: 6

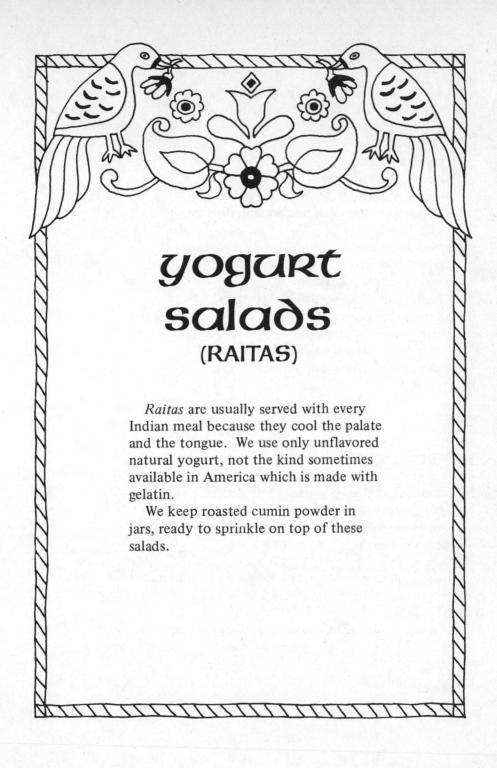

yogurt salads
(RAITAS)

Raitas are usually served with every Indian meal because they cool the palate and the tongue. We use only unflavored natural yogurt, not the kind sometimes available in America which is made with gelatin.

We keep roasted cumin powder in jars, ready to sprinkle on top of these salads.

Yogurt Salads

A variety of yogurt salads may be made by beating 2 cups of yogurt and adding any one of these items:

20 *pakoras*
2 bananas, sliced
½ cup boiled chickpeas
½ cup pomegranate seeds
½ cup grapes, stemmed and seeded, if necessary
½ cup raisins
½ cup diced apples
6 beets, boiled and sliced
½ cup chopped pineapple
1 fresh green chili, seeded and chopped
½ cup grated carrots
½ cup grated horseradish
¼ cup boiled, chopped cauliflower
½ cup boiled, chopped potatoes

Apple Yogurt

1 apple, peeled and cored
1 cup yogurt
1 tablespoon honey
sugar to taste

Grate the apple and squeeze the pulp in a square of cloth, or cut the apple into chunks, place it in blender and strain it. Discard the pulp in both methods. Use the juice.

Beat the yogurt with a fork. Add the juice of the apple, honey and sugar.

Chill.

Serves: 2

Carrot Yogurt

3 tablespoons carrot juice
1 cup yogurt
2 teaspoons lemon juice
1 tablespoon honey
sugar to taste

You can juice a carrot by using a centrifugal juicer which grates the vegetable and then whirls it around to separate the juice from the pulp, or you can grate the carrots, put the pulp in a muslin square or bag and squeeze the pulp with your hands.

Beat the yogurt with a fork and add 3 tablespoons of carrot juice and the rest of the ingredients. Stir and chill.

Serves: 2

Eggplant and Yogurt Salad *(Baigan Ka Raita)*

2 cups yogurt
1 cup boiled, mashed eggplant
salt to taste
1 teaspoon roasted powdered cumin seeds
1 teaspoon roasted powdered coriander seeds
2 roasted powdered red dried chilies
a few chopped mint leaves, for garnish

Beat the yogurt with a fork until it is smooth. Add the other ingredients except the mint. Chill until ready to serve. Garnish with mint leaves.

Serves: 6

Onion and Tomato Yogurt Salad *(Raita)*

2 cups yogurt
1 medium tomato, chopped
1 medium onion, chopped *or*
    4 green onions, chopped
salt to taste
½ fresh green chili, seeded and chopped
½ teaspoon cayenne pepper
½ teaspoon roasted cumin powder, for garnish
a few coriander leaves, chopped, for garnish

Beat the yogurt with a fork in a bowl until it is smooth. Combine with all the other ingredients except the garnish.

Pour into a small glass bowl and chill in the refrigerator. When ready to serve sprinkle cumin and coriander leaves over the top.

Serves: 8

Variations: Instead of tomato and onion, use 1 cucumber, peeled and grated, or use ½ lb. peeled, grated and boiled zucchini.

Potato and Yogurt Salad *(Aloo Ka Raita)*

2 cups yogurt
3 potatoes, boiled, peeled, chopped
1 teaspoon roasted, powdered cumin
salt to taste
1 fresh green chili, seeded and chopped
½ teaspoon cayenne pepper
a few mint leaves, chopped

Beat the yogurt with a fork. Add all the ingredients except the mint. Refrigerate and serve, garnished with mint leaves.

Serves: 6-8

Spinach Yogurt Salad *(Palak Ka Raita)*

2 cups yogurt
1 cup boiled, chopped spinach
salt to taste
1 teaspoon oil
1 teaspoon mustard seeds

Beat the yogurt with a fork in a bowl till smooth. Add the spinach and stir.

In a little pan, heat the oil, add the mustard seeds and fry till they pop. Pour over the salad. Stir and place in the refrigerator till cold.

Serves: 6

Tomato Yogurt

1 cup yogurt
1 tablespoon tomato juice
salt and pepper to taste
1 teaspoon roasted powdered cumin seeds

Mix all the ingredients and serve chilled.

Serves: 2

Fried Chickpea Balls and Yogurt Salad

Balls:

  1 cup chickpea flour
  ½ cup water
  pinch of salt
  pinch of cayenne pepper
  ½ cup oil for frying

Seasoned Yogurt:

  2 cups yogurt
  salt to taste
  1 teaspoon roasted, powdered cumin
  ½ teaspoon cayenne pepper
  a few coriander leaves, for garnish

For the Balls:

Mix chickpea flour with water, salt and cayenne. Blend well. Pour this batter through a wide meshed sieve so that drops the size of peas fall into the hot oil. As soon as they puff out, remove and drain on paper towels. Cool. They can be made ahead of time and stored in a container with a tight lid. You will need ½ cup of these for this salad.

For the Seasoned Yogurt:

Stir the yogurt with a fork. Add the seasonings and stir. Add the chickpea balls (½ cup) and stir gently. Put in refrigerator until ready to serve. Garnish with coriander leaves. If you like, sprinkle some more cumin powder on top.

  Serves: 6-8

Note: See page 35 for another yogurt salad, made with fritters instead of balls.

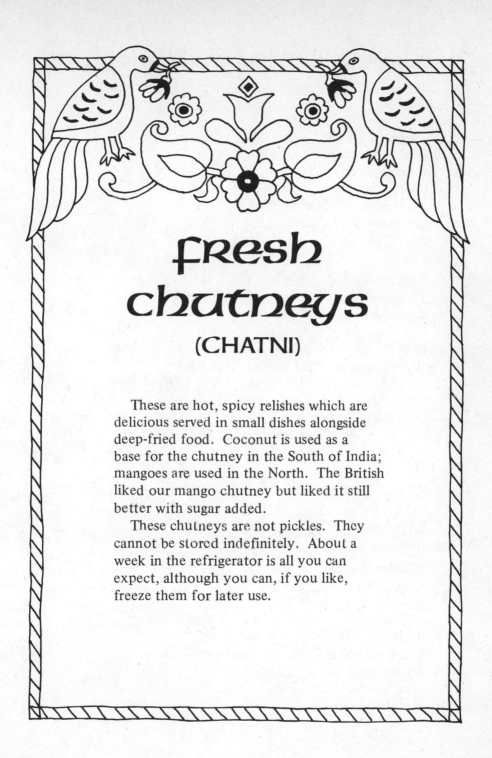

fResh chutneys
(CHATNI)

These are hot, spicy relishes which are delicious served in small dishes alongside deep-fried food. Coconut is used as a base for the chutney in the South of India; mangoes are used in the North. The British liked our mango chutney but liked it still better with sugar added.

These chutneys are not pickles. They cannot be stored indefinitely. About a week in the refrigerator is all you can expect, although you can, if you like, freeze them for later use.

Chutney for Rice Pancake I *(Dosa Chatni)*

The recipes on this page and the next are to be served with *dosas*.

2 tablespoons oil
8 dried red chilies
½ dried coconut, grated
¼ cup *urad dal*
2 tablespoons tamarind paste
salt to taste

Baghar:

1 tablespoon oil
1 teaspoon cumin seeds
2 dried red chilies, broken

Heat the oil in a skillet and fry the chilies, coconut and *urad dal* for a few minutes until coconut turns golden.

Put in blender with tamarind paste and salt. Grind. Remove to a small bowl.

Heat the oil and fry the cumin and red chilies till cumin seeds darken a bit. Pour over chutney and stir.

Chutney II *(Dosa Chatni)*

2 tablespoons oil
½ dried coconut, grated
4 red dried whole chilies
salt to taste
2 tablespoons tamarind paste
2 tablespoons chopped fresh coriander leaves
1 tablespoon yellow split peas
¼ cup water
1 cup yogurt

Baghar:

    1 tablespoon oil
    1 teaspoon mustard seeds

Heat oil in a skillet and roast the next 6 ingredients for a few minutes until coconut is light gold. Put in blender with water and yogurt. Grind. Place in a small bowl.

Make a *baghar* by frying mustard seeds in oil till they pop. Pour over chutney and stir.

Chutney III *(Dosa Chatni)*

    1 tablespoon oil
    2 teaspoons yellow split peas
    2 teaspoons *urad dal*
    ½ dried coconut, grated
    ¼ cup water
    1 inch piece ginger root
    12 curry leaves, optional
    6 fresh green chilies, seeded
    salt to taste

    1 tablespoon oil
    1 teaspoon mustard seeds

¼ cup yogurt
    2 teaspoons lemon juice
    1 teaspoon *sambhar* powder

Heat oil in a skillet and fry the split peas, *urad dal* and coconut until the coconut turns golden. Place in blender with water, ginger, curry leaves, chilies and salt. Grind to a smooth paste and place in a bowl.

Heat the oil and fry mustard seeds until they pop. Pour over chutney. Stir and let cool.

Add the yogurt, lemon juice and *sambhar* powder. Stir.

Coconut Chutney I *(Nariyal Chatni)*

This and the following two recipes are especially good served with Steamed Rice Cakes.

1 tablespoon oil
¼ dried coconut, grated
1 teaspoon *urad dal*
4 dried red chilies *or*
    4 fresh green chilies, seeded
2 tablespoons tamarind paste
salt to taste

Heat the oil in a skillet and fry the coconut and *urad dal* until coconut is golden. Place in blender with rest of ingredients and grind coarsely.

Cocunut Chutney II *(Nariyal Chatni)*

½ fresh coconut, grated
4 fresh green chilies, seeded
2 tablespoons chopped fresh mint or coriander leaves
salt to taste
1 teaspoon sugar
1 tablespoon tamarind paste or lemon juice
1 tablespoon roasted split peas
dash of water
1 cup yogurt

Combine the first seven ingredients and grind in a blender with a dash of water and yogurt.

Coconut Chutney III *(Nariyal Chatni)*

½ fresh coconut, grated
4 fresh green chilies, seeded and finely chopped
1 inch piece ginger root
2 cloves garlic
2 tablespoons *chanas,* roasted and shelled
1 teaspoon cumin seeds
salt to taste
1 cup yogurt

Baghar:

1 tablespoon oil
1 teaspoon black mustard seeds
1 teaspoon *urad dal*

Place the first seven ingredients in a blender and grind. Place in a bowl. Add yogurt and stir. Heat oil and fry mustard seeds and *urad dal.* Pour over chutney and stir.

Chili Chutney *(Hari Mirch Chatni)*

12 fresh green chilies, seeded and chopped
salt to taste
juice of 3 lemons
1 teaspoon roasted ground cumin seeds

Grind together in a blender. Good with rice dishes.

Chili Chutney I *(Lal Mirchi Chatni)*

½ cup dried red chilies
water to cover chilies
6 cloves of garlic
salt to taste
¼ cup yogurt

Soak the chilies in water for an hour. Drain. Grind together with garlic, salt and yogurt.

Chili Chutney II *(Lal Mirchi Chatni)*

5 lemons
12 dried red chilies
2 teaspoons cumin seeds
salt to taste
2 cloves garlic

Juice the lemons. Soak the chilies in the juice for 3 hours. Put in blender with cumin, salt and garlic. Grind.

Coriander Chutney *(Hara Dhaniya Chatni)*

2 cups chopped green coriander
1 teaspoon cayenne pepper
1 teaspoon salt
1 teaspoon roasted cumin seed, ground
1 teaspoon roasted coriander seeds, ground
1 tablespoon lemon juice
½ cup water

Grind all the ingredients in a blender.

Dal Chutney *(Dal Chatni)*

1 tablespoon oil
4 tablespoons pigeon peas *or*
  yellow split peas
2 fresh green chilies, seeded
salt to taste
2 tablespoons tamarind juice
2 tablespoons fresh coriander leaves, chopped
½ teaspoon mustard seeds

Baghar (see page 18):

1 tablespoon oil
½ teaspoon mustard seeds

Heat oil in heavy saucepan and roast the pigeon peas. Add all the ingredients except the *baghar*. Cool slightly, then grind in a blender. Place in a small bowl. Pour a *baghar* of mustard seeds over the chutney and mix thoroughly.

Ginger Chutney *(Sonth)*

8 oz. dried whole green mangoes
2 teaspoons cayenne pepper
1 cup molasses or brown sugar
1 quart water
6 teaspoons salt
½ cup sugar
2 teaspoons ground dried ginger
1 teaspoon *garam masala* powder
1 teaspoon powdered roasted cumin
2 teaspoons raisins

Put the mangoes, cayenne pepper and molasses in a saucepan. Add the water. Boil the mangoes until they soften. Blend the mixture. Add the rest of the ingredients and mix well.

If the chutney is too hot, either decrease the amount of cayenne to your taste or dilute the chutney with a little water.

Mango Chutney I *(Aam Chatni)*

1 tablespoon oil
1 teaspoon cumin seeds
1 teaspoon coriander seeds
2 red chilies, finely chopped
2 raw green mangoes, chopped
salt to taste
4 tablespoons fresh mint or coriander leaves, finely chopped
¼ cup water

Heat the oil in a frying pan. Roast the cumin and coriander seeds and the chilies for a few minutes. Remove and place in a blender with mangoes, salt, mint and water. Grind to a smooth paste.

Mango Chutney II *(Aam Chatni)*

2 green raw mangoes, chopped
4 tablespoons mint, finely chopped
salt to taste
2 fresh green chilies, seeded and chopped
¼ cup water

Blend all ingredients together with water to make a smooth consistency.

Mango or Apple Chutney
(Seb Ya Aam Ki Chatni)

This is a sweet chutney. Green apples may be substituted for the mangoes. Weigh the apples after you have peeled and cored them.

2 lbs. green half-ripe mangoes, peeled and cut into pieces
1 tablespoon salt for sprinkling
4 cups wine vinegar
3 cups sugar
1 cup raisins
2 tablespoons sliced ginger root
20 cloves garlic
1 tablespoon cayenne pepper
pinch of saffron (optional)
2 tablespoons salt

Before weighing mangoes, peel and cut them into pieces. Sprinkle 1 tablespoon of salt on mangoes and let stand overnight.

In the morning, squeeze out and discard the water.

Mix the mangoes with vinegar and the rest of the ingredients. Boil in a stainless steel pan until mixture thickens (about 1 hour). Keep stirring.

Remove from heat and cool 3-4 hours.

Put in jars and store in a cool place. Ready to eat immediately.

Note: Because of the sugar and vinegar this will keep longer than the other chutneys in this chapter.

Mint Chutney *(Podina Chatni)*

2 cups chopped mint
2 medium onions, chopped
1 teaspoon cumin seeds
1 fresh green chili, seeded and chopped
1 teaspoon sugar
1 teaspoon salt
1 tablespoon lemon juice
½ cup water

Put all ingredients in the blender and grind.

Onion Chutney *(Pyaaz Chatni)*

1 tablespoon oil
1 teaspoon cumin seeds
4 dried red chilies
1 tablespoon roasted sesame seeds
4 medium onions, chopped
salt to taste
1 teaspoon sugar
2 tablespoons tamarind juice

Baghar (see page 18):

1 tablespoon oil
½ teaspoon mustard seeds

In a small pan, heat oil. Add cumin seeds, chilies and sesame seeds and fry till sesame seeds are a little darker. Place in a blender. Add raw onions, salt, sugar and tamarind water. Grind. Remove to a small bowl. Make a *baghar* by frying oil and mustard seeds. Pour on chutney and stir.

Peanut Chutney *(Mungphalli Chatni)*

1 inch piece of tamarind
2 tablespoons water

1 tablespoon oil
1 teaspoon cumin seeds
3 dried red chilies
2 tablespoons tamarind juice
1 cup chopped mint leaves
½ cup roasted peanuts
salt to taste
1 teaspoon sugar

Baghar:

1 tablespoon oil
½ teaspoon mustard seeds
a few curry leaves, optional

Soak tamarind in water until soft and squeeze out the juice. Discard the pulp.

In a skillet, heat oil and add next four ingredients. Fry a few minutes.

Put in a blender with peanuts, salt and sugar. Grind. Remove to a small bowl.

Make a *baghar* by frying the mustard seeds and curry leaves. Pour over chutney and stir.

Variation: You can use roasted sesame seeds instead of the peanuts to make Sesame Seed Chutney *(Til).*

Plum Chutney *(Aloo Bukhara Chatni)*

This has a sweet-sour taste. It can be made only when the plums are in season. Any plum may be substituted that is not too sour or too sweet.

4 red plums, pitted and chopped
4 tablespoons fresh mint, chopped
2 green chilies, seeded and finely chopped *or*
   2 red chilies, crumbled
1 teaspoon sugar
salt to taste
1 teaspoon roasted cumin seeds
¼ cup water

Blend all ingredients together in a blender.

Tomato Chutney *(Tamatar Chatni)*

1 teaspoon oil
½ teaspoon cumin seeds
1 teaspoon chopped fresh ginger root
2 cloves garlic, chopped
1 medium onion, chopped
4 tomatoes, coarsely chopped
2 dried red chilies
1 tablespoon roasted sesame seeds
salt to taste
1 teaspoon sugar

Baghar:

1 tablespoon oil
½ teaspoon cumin seeds

Heat oil in a saucepan and fry cumin seeds till they darken a little. Add quickly, in order, one at a time the ginger, garlic, onion, tomatoes and red chilies. Cover and cook for 10 minutes over medium heat. Let cool slightly.

Place in blender with sesame seeds, salt and sugar. Blend till smooth. Place in a small bowl.

Fry the cumin seeds in hot oil till they change color. Pour the *baghar* over the chutney and stir.

Sweet and Sour Chutney

This chutney is a mixture of Indian and Chinese flavors.

½ cup tamarind paste
½ cup ketchup
1 inch piece fresh ginger root
6 cloves garlic
salt to taste
2 teaspoons sugar
2 teaspoons soy sauce

In blender combine all ingredients. If too thick, add a little water. Delicious with *samosas* and *pakoras*.

Yogurt Chutney *(Dahi Chatni)*

½ cup yogurt
4 cloves garlic
6 dried red chilies
salt to taste

Baghar:

1 tablespoon oil
1 teaspoon cumin seeds

Place in a blender the yogurt, garlic, red chilies and salt. Grind. Set aside. Heat oil and add cumin seeds. Fry till seeds change color slightly. Add the contents of the blender and cook for 5-10 minutes, uncovered.

pickles
(ACHAARS)

Pickles are an important element in Indian meals as a side dish for curries or as a substitute for curries. They are also the best way to preserve fruits and vegetables safely, without refrigeration. Pickles pickled properly can last up to a year.

As preservatives, we use oil, vinegar, lemon juice, salt or hot red peppers. Of these, oil pickles have the longest life. Our pickles can be hot, sweet, sour or salty.

We mix the pickles, being very careful to use absolutely dry, clean wooden or stainless steel spoons. Any bit of water (in vinegar or oil-based pickles) or foreign matter can spoil the pickles. Once they are mixed and placed in glass jars, we cover them tightly with a square of cloth and a string or elastic and place them in the sun to kill off any bacteria which would spoil the pickles.

Green Chili Pickle *(Hari Mirch Ka Achaar)*

These are wonderful.

20 green chilies, washed and dried
4 tablespoons mustard powder
2 teaspoons fenugreek powder
2 teaspoons asafetida
4 teaspoons turmeric powder
1 tablespoon salt
1 cup lemon juice
3 cups oil
2 teaspoons mustard seeds

Make a slit in the chilies. Mix all the powdered spices and place some inside each. Put them in a jar and after a week, add lemon juice. Heat the oil and add mustard seeds. Fry 2 minutes. Cool. Then add it to the pickle and stir.

Keep in an air-tight jar on the kitchen shelf or window where direct sunlight comes in. After 2 weeks it is ready to serve.

Green Chili Pickle *(Hari Mirchi Ka Achaar)*

This lasts only a month or two because it has water as a base instead of oil. These are ready to eat in 3 days.

2 cups water
12 whole fresh chilies
1 tablespoon salt
1 tablespoon coarsely ground cumin seeds
2 tablespoons coarsely ground mustard seeds
1 teaspoon fenugreek seeds

Bring water to a boil. Add chilies and salt and parboil. Take the chilies out of the water and make a slit in one side. Stuff them with the spices and drop them back into the water. Cool for 2 hours and then pour into a wide-mouth jar with a tight lid.

Sweet and Sour Lemon Pickle
(Neebu Ka Khatta Mitha Achaar)

4 lemons
2 cups sugar
2 tablespoons cayenne pepper
2 tablespoons turmeric powder
½ teaspoon asafetida
4 tablespoons salt

Wash and dry lemons. Cut each one into 4 pieces. Mix lemons and the rest of the ingredients. Put in a wide-mouth jar with a lid and keep in the sun for 15 days. This is ready to eat in 2 weeks.

Lemon Pickle (Hyderabadi Neebu Achaar)

12 lemons
salt to taste
2 teaspoons turmeric powder
12 fresh green chilies, seeded and cut into small pieces
2 cups oil, preferably corn oil
2 teaspoons crushed mustard seeds
2 teaspoons fenugreek seeds
2 teaspoons crushed cumin seeds
2 teaspoons cayenne pepper

Wash and dry the lemons. Cut into small pieces. Add salt, turmeric and chilies and stir. Put in a wide-mouth jar. For 3 days, keep it in a warm place or where the sunlight comes in all day. Shake the bottle every day.

On the fourth day, heat the oil, then remove from heat. After the oil has cooled down, add the mustard, fenugreek, cumin seeds and cayenne pepper to the oil. Finally add the lemons. Stir. Let the pickle stand in the kitchen for 2 hours until it is completely cooled.

Mix it well with a dry wooden spoon. Ladle into jars and let it sit in the sunlight or any warm place 3 days longer.

Lemon and Green Chili Pickles
(Neebu Aur Hari Mirch Achaar)

This pickle is a combination of chopped lemon and chilies and ginger in an oil base, heavily seasoned with garlic and spices.

Pickles:

12 lemons, cut into small pieces
6 fresh green chilies, seeded and chopped
1 tablespoon fresh chopped ginger root
4 tablespoons salt

Oil Base:

2 cups oil
12 cloves garlic, crushed
2 tablespoons cayenne pepper
2 tablespoons roasted fenugreek seeds, coarsely crushed
2 tablespoons roasted mustard seeds coarsely crushed
2 tablespoons roasted cumin seeds, coarsely crushed

For the Pickles:

Mix the lemons, chilies, ginger and salt and place them in a jar. Set the jar in the sun for 3 days.

For the Base:

On the third day, heat the oil. Cool for 2 hours. Add the spices and stir.

Combine the lemon mixture and the oil mixture. The oil should cover the lemons. If not, heat more oil, let it cool completely and add it.

Put in a wide-mouth jar and place in the sun for 7 days. Shake the bottle every day to mix the spices.

Sweet Mango Pickle *(Aam Ka Mittha Achaar)*

This is a pickle of mangoes in sugar and vinegar, made hot with cayenne.

12 raw green mangoes, peeled and chopped
sugar (equal amount as mangoes, using the same measuring cup)
4 bay leaves
1 teaspoon salt
2 teaspoons cumin seeds
1 teaspoon fenugreek seeds
2 teaspoons cayenne pepper
1 teaspoon onion seeds
1 teaspoon peppercorns
1 teaspoon black cumin seeds
1 cup vinegar

Combine all ingredients except vinegar in a saucepan. Simmer for about 1 hour, stirring frequently. Let cool.

Pour into a large jar. Stir in vinegar and cover with a tight lid.

Mango Pickle
(Aam, Chanas and Besan Gatta Achaar)

This pickle has balls of grated mango and chickpea flour in an oil sauce which contains spices and whole chickpeas.

Chickpea Flour Balls:

2 half-ripe mangoes, peeled and grated
½ cup water for dough
2 tablespoons ground cumin seeds
2 teaspoons cayenne pepper
1 tablespoon *garam masala* powder
1 teaspoon salt
2 cups chickpea flour
2 cups oil for frying

Mango Pickle:

6 raw, slightly under-ripe mangoes
½ cup salt
2 cups oil
1 tablespoon cumin seeds
1 tablespoon onion seeds
1 teaspoon asafetida
1 tablespoon mustard seeds
1 tablespoon fenugreek seeds
1 tablespoon anise seeds
1 tablespoon cayenne pepper
1 teaspoon turmeric powder
2 tablespoons salt
1 cup boiled chickpeas

For the Chickpea Flour Balls:

Mix everything together except the oil for frying. Knead into a stiff dough. Form into small balls. Boil in 3 cups water for 10 minutes. Remove balls from water and let cool.

Using a thread held in both hands, slice the balls into halves. Deep-fry them and set aside.

For the Mango Pickle:

Wash the mangoes and cut them into small pieces. Sprinkle with half a cup of salt and let stand overnight. In the morning, drain and discard water.

Heat the oil in a wok and fry the cumin seeds, onion seeds and asafetida for a few minutes.

Add the drained mangoes and cook until tender. Remove from heat.

Add the other spices and salt. Stir. Be sure the oil covers the mangoes. Add the chickpea flour balls and chickpeas and let cool.

Store in a wide-mouth jar with a tight lid.

Mango Pickle in Oil *(Aam Ka Achaar)*

This is a very hot pickle made of long pieces of mango preserved in oil and spices.

12 raw green mangoes
½ cup salt
4 cups oil
6 whole red chilies
2 teaspoons peppercorns
4 bay leaves
2 teaspoons coriander seeds
2 teaspoons cumin seeds
2 teaspoons mustard seeds
2 teaspoons turmeric powder
½ cup vinegar

Wash and cut each of the mangoes into 8 long pieces. Sprinkle with salt and let stand overnight in a bowl. The next morning drain the mangoes and discard salty water. Set the mangoes aside.

Boil the oil and cool slightly.

Put the spices in a blender and grind them coarsely. Add the spices and vinegar to the oil. Set aside to cool.

When oil is completely cool, pour it over the mangoes. Stir carefully with a clean, dry spoon and place in a wide-mouth jar with a clean cloth tied over the top. Place in a sunny window or outside in an unshaded spot every day for 15 days.

9 Jewel Chutney *(Naw Rattan Chatni)*

This lasts indefinitely. There are 9 ingredients of the same weight; hence, the name.

1 lb. peeled, raw, green mangoes, cut into pieces
1 lb. garlic
1 lb. onions, chopped
1 lb. dried red chilies
1 lb. brown sugar or molasses
1 lb. coriander seeds
1 lb. peeled, fresh ginger root
1 lb. salt
8 cups wine vinegar

The mangoes should be weighed after they are peeled and chopped. Similarly, the garlic and the onions.

Lay out 7 bowls. Place each of the first 7 ingredients in a bowl and cover with a cup of vinegar. Let stand 2 hours.

Grind each separately in a blender.

Combine all 7 bowls into 1 big bowl. Stir and add salt. Put through blender once more.

Add last cup of vinegar. Stir and store in an airtight jar.

Notes: Not a single drop of water should touch this chutney or the whole thing will spoil. You can make this chutney in any quantity you like, so long as the ingredients are of equal weight.

Onion Pickle *(Chote Pyaaz Ka Achaar)*

1 lb. small onions
2 tablespoons mustard seeds
20 cloves garlic
1 tablespoon salt
4 tablespoons cayenne pepper
2 tablespoons turmeric powder
2 cups oil
3 cups water

Peel the onions and place in a large mixing bowl. Grind the mustard seeds in a coffee grinder or blender. Then grind the garlic and add both to the onions. Mix in the salt, cayenne pepper, turmeric powder and oil. Add the water and mix well. Keep in a jar for a week and shake it daily. Can be served after a week.

Note: 1 lb. of carrots or 1 lb. of cauliflower can be substituted for the onions.

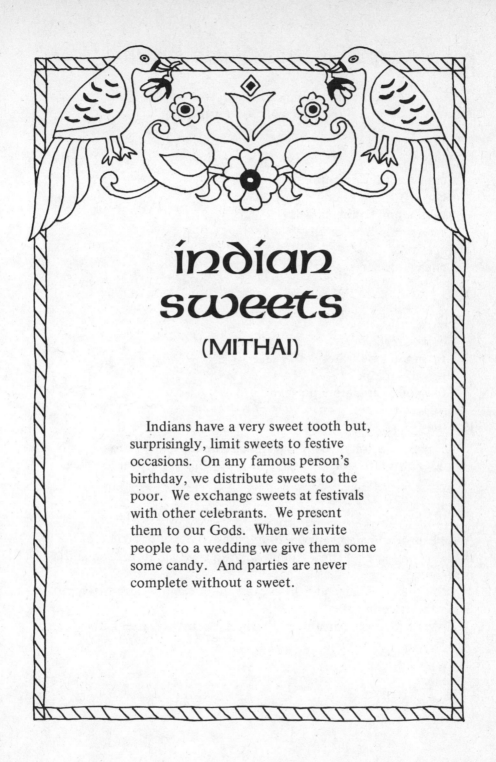

indian sweets
(MITHAI)

Indians have a very sweet tooth but, surprisingly, limit sweets to festive occasions. On any famous person's birthday, we distribute sweets to the poor. We exchange sweets at festivals with other celebrants. We present them to our Gods. When we invite people to a wedding we give them some some candy. And parties are never complete without a sweet.

Rose Syrup Milk Balls *(Gulab Jamun)*

This is the most popular Indian sweet. We serve the balls in bowls with several teaspoons of rose syrup.

Dough:

2 cups instant dried milk powder
1 cup self-rising flour
1 tablespoon baking powder
1 tablespoon *ghee* or oil
1 cup milk
2 cups oil for frying

Syrup:

2 cups sugar
1 cup water
1 teaspoon rose water
pinch of saffron
1 teaspoon cardamom powder

For the Dough:

To make the dough, combine all ingredients, except the oil for frying. Form into small balls and deep-fry in hot oil over low heat until they turn reddish brown.

For the Syrup:

Boil sugar and water for 15-20 minutes to the consistency of a thin syrup. Let cool for 10 minutes. Add rose water, saffron and cardamom.

Drop the fried balls into the syrup and let them absorb the syrup. Serve these warm.

If you wish, you can stuff raisins in the center of each ball before you fry it.

Yields: 20-24

Milk Balls in Sugar Syrup *(Rasgulla)*

This is a light dessert, very easy to digest, with no fat in it whatsoever. The balls can be prepared another way: flattened, boiled and served with a thick milk sauce, *rabri* (see page 200); it then becomes a dish called *Ras-Malai.*

5 cups milk
2 tablespoons lemon juice *or*
   2 tablespoons white vinegar
½ teaspoon all-purpose flour
a few sugar cubes

Sugar Syrup:

2 cups sugar
1 cup water
1 teaspoon rose water

Bring the milk to a boil. Remove from heat and add lemon juice or vinegar. Stir. When milk curdles, put it into a cotton square you have previously wet and wrung out. Tie the corners of the square so that you have a bag and let it drip (in a sieve placed over a saucepan) for 2 hours. Squeeze the bag so that any remaining fluid will be forced out of the cheese.

Take the cheese out of the bag, place in a bowl and add flour. Knead thoroughly.

Form small balls. Break sugar cubes with a small hammer or the flat edge of a cleaver into 3 or 4 pieces each. Put a piece into the center of each ball.

Boil sugar and water for 15-20 minutes to the consistency of a thin syrup. Pour half the syrup out into a bowl. Bring the remaining syrup to a boil and drop the balls in gently, one by one. Boil until the balls float to the surface. Remove with a slotted spoon and place them in the syrup reserved in a bowl. Let cool.

Add rose water and stir gently. Serve either drained on a plate or with a bit of syrup in a bowl.

Yields: 16-20

Sugar Coated Cookies *(Sakkarpaara)*

These are rolled bread discs, cut in diamond shapes, deep fat fried and dipped in sugar syrup.

Dough:

2 cups all purpose white flour
4 tablespoons *ghee*
½ cup water
2 cups oil for frying

For Sugar Coating Syrup:

2 cups sugar
½ cup water

Mix flour with *ghee*. Add water to make a stiff dough. Roll out into a thick flat disc like a *chappati,* about 6 inches in diameter. Cut diamond shapes with a knife and deep-fry them. Drain on a paper towel.

Make a sugar syrup by boiling sugar and water for 20-25 minutes. After frying all the cookies, glaze them by dropping a few at a time in the sugar syrup. Take them out and cool on a rack.

These can be stored in a jar for about 2-4 weeks.

Yields: 40-50

Indian Sweets in Sugar Syrup *(Jalebis)*

These are delicious and light. If the pretzel shapes don't come out right, close your eyes and eat them anyway. They are a little sticky because the sugar syrup never dries.

Dough:

 2 cups all purpose white flour
 1½ cups water
 1 teaspoon yogurt

Syrup:

 3 cups sugar
 2 cups water
 a pinch of saffron powder
 1 tablespoon lemon juice

 2 cups oil for frying

Combine flour, water and yogurt to make a thick batter. Let stand, covered, for 24 hours in a warm place to ferment and rise.

Boil sugar and water till it is a thin syrup, about 25 minutes. Add lemon juice and reduce heat to a simmer. Cool slightly.

Heat oil in a wok. Take an empty plastic ketchup or mustard bottle which has a small funnel-like opening at the top. Fill this with the batter. Squeeze out the batter in the figure 8. Fry until they are crisp and pale brown. Take them out with a spatula with holes in it so that the *jalebis* drain. Drop them into the warm syrup so that the syrup will penetrate the hollow *jalebis*. Remove and put on a plate.

Serves: 12-16

Fried Flour Fritters in Syrup *(Balushahi)*

These, unlike the preceeding *jalebis,* are not made of fermented dough. They are very heavy and very sweet.

Dough:

    2 cups flour
    3 tablespoons *ghee*
    1 teaspoon cinnamon
    1 teaspoon anise seed
    ½ cup water
    2 cups oil for frying

Syrup:

    5 cups sugar
    3 cups water

Combine flour and *ghee.* Add cinnamon, anise seeds and water to make a soft dough. Divide into 12 equal rounds and flatten with your fingers into circular shapes about 2½ inches in diameter. Make a dent in the center with your thumb.

Heat oil and deep-fry, one or two at a time, and drain on a paper towel. Make a thick syrup by boiling sugar and water for 30 minutes. Drop the fried fritters into the syrup and let soak for ½ hour. Take them out and place them on a flat plate.

Yields: 12

Indian Pancakes in Syrup *(Malpua)*

These are tasty, sticky crepes which are made for festivals.

Syrup:

> 2 cups sugar
> 1 cup water
> 1 teaspoon rose water

Dough:

> 2 cups all-purpose white flour
> 1 cup milk
> ¾ cup sugar
> 1 tablespoon almonds, blanched and sliced
> 1 tablespoon fresh coconut, cut in thin slices
> 1 cup *ghee* for frying

Boil the sugar and water for 15-20 minutes until it is the consistency of a thin syrup. Remove from heat and stir in rose water. Set aside.

Mix the ingredients for the dough (except the *ghee* for frying) together with a fork. Place the dough in a bowl, cover it and set it out overnight on the kitchen counter. It will ferment and rise by morning.

Heat a cast-iron griddle. Pour a teaspoonful of *ghee* on the griddle. Pour a spoonful of batter and quickly spread it into a large circle with a spatula. Pour a little *ghee* around the pancake and let it cook. Turn the pancake over and cook the other side. Make the rest of the pancakes in this manner until the batter is used up. Stack the pancakes.

Roll the pancakes like crepes and pour the sugar syrup over them.

Serves: 10-12

Indian Sweet Bread

This is akin to shortbread, delicately spiced.

2 cups all purpose white flour
1 lb. powdered sugar
1 teaspoon cardamom powder
2 teaspoons sesame seeds
2 cups *ghee*
a pinch of saffron dissolved in 1 tablespoon milk
a few slivered almonds
a few slivered pistachios

Sift the flour and sugar. Add cardamom and sesame seeds. Mix.
Pour warm *ghee* over dry mixture and work with a wooden spoon
or your hands into a smooth, soft dough.
Divide into 20 balls and put them on a cookie sheet. Flatten with
your hand into 4 inch rounds. With a fork, make a pattern on the
rotis. Trace the lines you have made with saffron and milk mixture.
Decorate with nuts and bake at 350 degrees for 10 minutes.
Cool on a cookie sheet. Remove carefully with a spatula.
Yields: 20

Chickpea Flour Sweet Balls *(Besan Ke Laddoo)*

These are like rich butter cookies.

½ cup *ghee*
1 cup chickpea flour
1 cup sugar
¼ teaspoon cardamom powder
1 tablespoon chopped cashews

Melt *ghee* in a heavy saucepan and add flour. Stir and fry till
brown. Stir in sugar, cardamom and cashews. If mixture is too
crumbly, add a little milk. When mixture is cool enough to handle,
roll into balls.
Yields: 12-14 balls

Carrot Pudding I *(Gajjar Kheer)*

4 carrots, grated
4 cups milk
1 cup sugar
½ teaspoon vanilla

In a saucepan boil carrots in milk for 20 minutes. Add sugar and boil 10 more minutes. Remove from heat and add vanilla. Stir. Serve in bowls either warm or cold.

Serves: 8

Carrot Pudding II *(Gajjar Kheer)*

This is very fruity—richer and more filling than the preceding recipe.

8 cashews
1 tablespoon *ghee*
6 dates
1 banana
1 cup grated carrots
1 cup milk
1 cup sugar
pinch of cardamom powder

Fry the cashews in *ghee* until they are golden. Chop them into small pieces. Set aside.

Pit the dates. Peel the banana. Cut both fruits into small pieces. Set aside.

Steam the grated carrots over boiling water.

Place in a heavy bottomed saucepan with milk and sugar. Boil for a few minutes. Remove from heat.

Add the fruit, cashews and cardamom. Cook a little longer, stirring constantly, until mixture becomes a solid mass. Serve in small portions on dessert plates.

Cauliflower Pudding *(Gobi Ki Kheer)*

Unless people have watched you prepare this dessert, they will not be able to guess what's in it.

½ medium head of cauliflower
3 tablespoons *ghee*
4 cups milk
1 cup sugar
½ cup raisins
1 tablespoon dried, grated coconut
¼ cup ground almonds
1 teaspoon *kewra* essence or rose water
12 roasted pistachios, sliced

Cut cauliflower into small pieces and brown in *ghee*. Remove from frying pan and set aside.

In a heavy-bottomed saucepan boil the milk and sugar. Add the cauliflower and boil until it becomes thick. Keep stirring. Mash the cauliflower with the back of your spoon.

Add raisins, coconut and almonds and cook 5 minutes more. Keep stirring. Pour in a serving bowl, add *kewra* essence or rose water. Stir. Sprinkle pistachios on top. Serve at room temperature.

Serves: 8

Ghee Pudding *(Mohan Bhog)*

This is a thick, buttery pudding, flavored lightly with saffron and cardamom.

¾ cup *ghee*
1 cup all-purpose white flour
4 cups milk, divided
2 cups sugar
¼ cup raisins
1 teaspoon cardamom powder
a pinch of saffron
4 edible silver leaves (optional)

In a heavy saucepan, heat ¼ cup ghee. Add flour and fry till brown. Add 2 cups of milk and cook till thick.

Add 2 more cups of milk, raisins, cardamom and saffron. Cook and stir for 2-3 minutes.

Add the rest of the *ghee* and cook several minutes more.

Place in serving dish and garnish with silver leaves. Serve warm or at room temperature.

Serves: 8

Egg Pudding *(Egg Halva)*

This is very easy to make.

6 eggs, separated
1 cup sugar
½ cup *ghee*
4 cups milk
½ cup heavy cream
12 almonds, blanched and sliced
¼ cup raisins
a pinch of saffron

Beat egg whites in a bowl until stiff. Add the yolks, one at a time, and beat. Add sugar and beat. Add milk and beat. This is simpler if you use an electric mixer.

Stir the *ghee* into the egg mixture. Transfer to a heavy bottomed saucepan and cook over low heat, stirring constantly. When mixture is like scrambled eggs, add cream, almonds, raisins and saffron.

Cook for 5 minutes more over low heat, stirring constantly. Serve warm or cold.

Serves: 12

Pumpkin Pudding *(Kaddu Halwa)*

2 cups pumpkin, cut into small pieces
1 cup water
1 cup sugar
¼ cup *ghee* or butter
½ cup instant dry milk powder
a pinch of saffron
a few edible silver leaves (optional)

In a saucepan with a heavy bottom, cook the pumpkin with water. When it is soft, add sugar and boil. When the water evaporates, add ghee and cook 15 minutes more, stirring constantly. Add the dry milk and continue to cook, stirring constantly.

Remove from heat and stir in the saffron. Place in serving dish and decorate with silver leaves (optional). Serve warm.

Serves: 12

Rice Pudding I *(Chawal Kheer)*

This is rice pudding made more exotic by the addition of raisins, almonds and flavorings.

4 cups milk
1 cup raw *patna* rice or any other rice
½ cup water
1 cup sugar
½ cup raisins
¼ cup almonds, blanched, sliced or ground
2 teaspoons rose water
1 teaspoon cardamom powder
edible silver leaves, (optional)

In a heavy saucepan, bring the milk to a boil and add rice and water. Cook until rice is soft. Add sugar and continue cooking for 10 minutes.

Remove from heat. Add raisins, almonds and rose water. Pour into a big bowl. Sprinkle cardamom powder on top and decorate with silver paper. Serve warm or cold.

Serves: 8

Rice Pudding II *(Phirni)*

In North India, on a special night in October when the moon is at its fullest, people prepare this dish and set it outside in the moonlight in unglazed clay bowls for the gods to make nectar of. I remember how exciting it was for me as a child to eat my nectar at breakfast the following morning.

Because we use rice flour here instead of whole rice, you will not be able to distinguish the rice in this pudding.

4 cups milk
½ cup rice flour
½ cup water
1 cup sugar
2 tablespoons raisins
2 teaspoons rose water
1 teaspoon cardamom powder
12 almonds, blanched and sliced
12 sliced pistachios
sheets of silver paper (optional)

Bring milk to a boil in a heavy saucepan. Add rice flour and water and stir. Boil for 10 minutes. Keep stirring.

Add the sugar and cook, stirring constantly, until mixture becomes thick.

Remove from heat and add raisins and rose water. Stir. Pour into individual bowls and sprinkle with cardamom and nuts. Arrange silver leaves on top. Serve either hot or very cold.

Serves: 10

Semolina Pudding *(Sooji Kheer)*

This is a simple pudding, quite sweet with a few raisins added for intense pockets of flavor.

2 tablespoons butter or *ghee*
1 cup semolina (Cream of Wheat)
6 cups milk
1½ cups sugar
2 teaspoons raisins
1 teaspoon cardamom powder

Melt the butter and fry the semolina briefly, but do not let it brown. (This will enhance the flavor of the pudding.)
Add milk and boil 10 minutes. Keep stirring.
Add sugar and raisins and boil 5 more minutes.
Pour into individual bowls and sprinkle cardamom powder on top. Serve warm or cold.

Serves: 8-10

Vermicelli Pudding *(Sevian Ki Kheer)*

This is a Muslim speciality, prepared on their Idd day. You can see the vermicelli in the finished pudding suspended like tiny threads.

2 tablespoons *ghee*
¾ cup very fine vermicelli
4 cups milk
1 cup sugar
1 cup dry milk powder
2 teaspoons rose water *or*
   1 teaspoon *kewra* essence
1 teaspoon cardamom powder
a pinch of saffron
½ cup raisins
12 almonds, peeled and sliced
12 pistachios, sliced
a few silver leaves (optional)

Heat *ghee*. Break the vermicelli into small pieces and fry. When golden brown add the milk and bring to a boil. Add the sugar and continue cooking. After 10 minutes add the dry milk powder. Cook until it thickens. Add the rose water or *kewra* essence, cardamom, saffron and raisins. Pour into a serving dish and sprinkle nuts on top. Decorate with silver leaf (optional). Serve warm or cold.

Serves: 8-10

Zucchini Pudding *(Lauki Halwa)*

5 cups milk
4 cups zucchini, peeled and grated
1½ cups sugar
½ cup *ghee* or butter
20 almonds, blanched and sliced
½ cup raisins
1 teaspoon cardamom powder
a few silver leaves

Bring milk to a boil in a heavy saucepan. Add zucchini and boil until the milk appears to be absorbed.

Add sugar and cook, stirring constantly for about 10 minutes. Add the *ghee* and stir.

Cook over low heat until mixture thickens and starts to draw away from sides of pan. Remove from heat.

Add nuts and raisins and stir. Place in a serving bowl and sprinkle with cardamom. Decorate with silver leaves. This should always be served warm. You can substitute carrots for the zucchini.

Serves: 8-10

Almond Dessert *(Badaam Ka Halwa)*

This is somewhat like fudge or halvah.

2 cups almonds
water to cover
½ cup butter or *ghee*
¼ cup warm water
1 cup sugar
½ cup instant dry milk powder
a few chopped pistachios

Soak almonds in water to cover for 2 hours. Drain. Peel them and grind them to a fine paste in a blender.

Heat butter or *ghee* and fry the almond paste till it is brown. Add warm water and sugar and boil till water is evaporated.

Add the dry milk and cook 5-10 minutes more until the butter separates.

Put on a plate, flatten with your hand and arrange pistachios on top. Serve in small portions on dessert plates, at room temperature.

Serves: 8

Milk Dessert *(Rabri)*

This can be used frozen for Indian Ice Cream (see page 205).

8 cups milk
2 cups sugar
½ cup raisins
¼ cup fresh grated coconut
½ cup almonds, blanched and ground
1 teaspoon *kewra* essence or rose water
1 teaspoon cardamom powder

Bring milk to a boil in a wok. Let it boil for 1-2 hours, or until it becomes thick. Keep stirring so that the milk doesn't burn.

Add sugar and continue cooking until mixture becomes the consistency of pancake batter. Remove from heat.

Add raisins, coconut and almonds. Stir. Then add the *kewra* or rose water and cardamom.

This can be served either hot or cold, in tiny bowls.

Serves: 10

Semolina Dessert *(Sooji Ka Halwa)*

This is the consistency of a moist, heavy cake.

½ cup *ghee* or butter
1 cup semolina
2 cups milk
¾ cup sugar
12 almonds, blanched and sliced
¼ cup raisins
a pinch of saffron

In a wok heat *ghee* and fry semolina briefly. Be careful not to let the semolina get brown. Add milk and continue cooking for 8 minutes.

Add the sugar and boil until *ghee* separates. Remove from heat.

Add almond slices and raisins. Stir. Pour on a lightly greased plate, flatten with your hand and cut. Serve hot or cold.

Serves: 6

Yogurt Dessert *(Shrikhand)*

This is wonderful served ice cold on a hot summer day. It is a little like ricotta cheese with almonds, pistachios and spices added.

    4 cups yogurt
    1 cup sugar
    2 tablespoons almonds, blanched and sliced
    a few sliced pistachios
    ½ cup raisins
    a dash of cinnamon powder
    a pinch of nutmeg powder
    1 teaspoon cardamom powder
    ½ teaspoon saffron

Place yogurt in a damp cheesecloth bag. Tie it and elevate it so that it can drip (the spout of the kitchen sink is useful). After most of the water has dripped out, squeeze the bag.

Take out the curds and place in bowl. Mix to form a smooth paste and add rest of ingredients. Stir. Serve cold in small bowls.

Serves: 6

Bengali Coconut and Milk Sweet
(Nariyal Sandesh)

This is a delicious coconut candy.

meat from 1 medium-sized coconut
3 cups instant milk powder
2½ cups sugar
1 teaspoon vanilla *or* rose water
1 tablespoon *ghee*
24 raisins

Grate coconut. Mix it with milk powder and sugar. Place in a heavy saucepan and cook, stirring constantly, until very thick. Remove from heat. Add vanilla and *ghee* and mix well. Make small balls, flatten each with your hand and decorate with a raisin.

Yields: 24

Semolina Sweet Balls *(Sooji Ke Laddoo)*

These are like the coconut candy, but more substantial because of the addition of semolina. It is also nutritious. We make these every week and store them in cookie jars.

½ cup *ghee* or corn oil
2 cups semolina (Cream of Wheat)
2 cups sugar
½ cup fresh grated coconut
¼ cup almonds, blanched and sliced
2 teaspoons rose water
1 tablespoon cardamom powder
½ cup raisins
½ cup cold milk

Heat *ghee* in a wok; add semolina and fry until golden. Remove from heat. Add sugar, coconut, almonds, rose water, cardamom, and raisins. Pour cold milk in slowly and start mixing. The hot mixture and cold milk helps to form firm balls. Place on a plate to cool and dry.

Yields: 24

Indian Toffee *(Barfi)*

This is the toffee the British love so well. You can really get your teeth into this.

½ cup sugar
½ cup water
¼ can condensed milk
1 cup chopped nuts
¾ cup bread crumbs
1 tablespoon butter
a few drops of vanilla

Combine the sugar and water and bring to a boil. Remove from heat. Add the rest of the ingredients and mix well until mixture is thick and dough-like. While hot, roll out with a rolling pin on a greased surface. Cut into squares immediately.

Almond Toffee *(Badaam Barfi)*

This is a soft toffee.

¼ cup water
½ cup sugar
1 cup almonds, blanched and ground
1 cup powdered milk

Make a thin syrup with water and sugar by boiling them for 15-20 minutes. Remove from heat. Add almonds and powdered milk. Make into a dough. Roll out on a greased surface and cut into desired shapes.

Yields: 24

Coconut Toffee *(Coconut Barfi)*

All candies made with fresh coconut are heavenly.

meat from 2 coconuts
4 cups sugar
4½ cups milk
1 tablespoon *ghee*
6 edible silver leaves (optional)

Cut the coconut meat into small pieces and grind in a blender. Set aside.

Combine sugar and milk in a wok and simmer over low heat for 5 minutes. Add the coconut and simmer until mixture solidifies.

Spread on a greased cookie sheet. When toffee is cool, cut it into diamonds and decorate with silver leaf.

Instant Indian Ice Cream *(Quick Kulfi)*

Faluda Sauce:

    1-2 tablespoons vermicelli
    1 cup water
    ½ cup sugar
    a pinch of saffron

Ice Cream:

    1 pint vanilla ice cream
    ½ cup blanched, chopped almonds
    ¼ cup pistachios
    ½ teaspoon saffron powder absorbed in a little water
    2 teaspoons cardamom powder

For the Sauce:

Boil the vermicelli in water and sugar. When vermicelli is soft, remove from heat and add saffron. Set aside.

For the Ice Cream:

Soften ice cream 1 hour. Mix in the rest of the ingredients and freeze in small bowls. Serve with Faluda sauce.

Serves: 6

Indian Ice Cream *(Kulfi)*

Make a *rabri* (see page 200), add ½ cup of nuts and freeze in ice cube trays covered with aluminum foil. When *kulfi* is frozen, slice it and serve with Faluda sauce.

Mango Ice Cream

Excellent for big parties as it can be made in advance. Applesauce can be substituted for the mango.

1 pint vanilla ice cream
1   can mango pulp
½ cup toasted unsalted almonds
1 teaspoon cardamom powder

Soften ice cream on the kitchen counter for about 1 hour. Fold in the mango pulp, almonds and cardamom powder. Freeze.

Serves: 6-8

Almond Drink *(Thandai Sherbet)*

We don't have fruit juices in India. We drink mixtures like this instead.

8 cups sugar
4 cups water
½ cup almonds, soaked overnight, drained and ground
½ cup poppyseeds, soaked overnight, drained and ground
4 tablespoons cardamom powder
10 black peppercorns, ground
½ cup peeled melon seeds, dried and ground

Boil the water and sugar 15 minutes. Add the rest of the ingredients and boil 20 minutes more. Cool and strain. Pour into bottles and refrigerate. To serve, use 2 tablespoons of syrup to a glass of water and stir.

Watermelon Sherbet *(Tarbuz Ka Sherbet)*

In the streets of India, men trundle around little carts, selling this in glasses.

1 small ripe watermelon
2 cups water
4 tablespoons sugar
a few drops of rose water
1 teaspoon cardamom powder

Cut watermelon meat into small pieces. Mix with water and add all remaining ingredients. Fill a glass with crushed ice and pour in the watermelon sherbet. Mix and eat with a spoon.

Mango Drink I *(Aam Ka Sherbet)*

The taste of this is unusual, but people tend to like it.

2 raw green mangoes, peeled and sliced
water to cover
4 teaspoons sugar
1½ cups milk
1 cup water

Boil the mangoes in water till they are mushy. Strain, using a little pressure. Discard the pulp. You should have 1½ cups of mango juice.
Add the milk gradually, then the sugar. Stir and chill.

Mango Drink II *(Aam Ka Sherbet)*

20 almonds, soaked 1 hour in water
20 raisins
3 ripe mangoes
2 cups cold water
sugar to taste
a pinch of salt
1 pint vanilla ice cream

Remove the skins of the almonds. Grind almonds and raisins in blender to form a smooth paste.
Broil or bake the mangoes until they are soft. Take out of the oven and let cool.
Squeeze out the ripe mango juice. Mix with cold water, almond-raisin paste, sugar and salt. Beat well with a whisk.
Chill and serve in a tall glass with a scoop of vanilla ice cream.

Coconut Milk Shake *(Nariyal Ka Sherbet)*

2 cups milk
1 cup coconut milk (see page 19)
sugar to taste
2 tablespoons whipped cream
sweetened canned cherries or fresh sweet cherries

Combine milk, coconut milk and sugar. Mix in a blender and chill.
Pour in glasses and top with whipped cream and cherries.

Guava Jelly *(Amrud Ki Jelly)*

This jelly is very good spread on hot buttered toast. Passion fruit may be substituted for the guavas.

1 lb. unpeeled, chopped guavas
5 cups water
2 cups sugar
3 teaspoons butter
4 tablespoons lemon juice

Boil the chopped guavas in water until soft. Tie in a muslin cloth and let it drip into a bowl overnight. Squeeze the bag, boil the strained juice for about half an hour or until it thickens. Add the sugar and cook for another half hour. Add the butter and lemon juice. Pour into sterilized jelly glasses and seal with paraffin.

the finale
(PAAN)

Betel leaf is usually served at the end of an Indian meal and at weddings and parties. The betel plant is a creeper which has broad leaves like the money plant.

We prepare the *paan* this way. We wash each leaf carefully and dry it. Then we mix spices like *katha*, cardamom and anise with lime paste *(choona)*, grated coconut, different kinds of betel nuts *(suparies)* and small bits of sugar candy.

We place this mixture in the leaf and then fold the leaf into a triangular envelope, with a clove placed in the center to secure it. We keep them fresh on ice with rose petals.

You can buy *paan* on every street corner in India. They really help in the digestion of heavy foods and they also refresh one's mouth. If anyone ever offers you a *paan*, be sure to try it.

glossary

Aam, ripe mango fruit
Adrak, fresh ginger root
Ajwain, carom seeds, lovage
Akrot, walnut
Aloo, potato
Aloo Bukhara, plum
Amrud, guava
Anaaj, grains
Anaar Ka Daana, pomegranate seeds
Anda, egg
Angoor, grapes
Annanas, pineapple
Atta, whole wheat flour

Badaam, almonds
Bajera, millet
Baingan, eggplant
Beej, seeds
Besan, chickpea flour
Bhaat, cooked rice
Bhindi, okra
Bund Gobi, cabbage

Chaach, buttermilk
Chakla, pastry rolling board
Chana, chickpea

Chana Dal, split peas
Chappati, flat whole wheat bread
Chasni, syrup
Chawal, rice
Cheeni, sugar
Chola, garbanzo
Chukandar, red beet
Chulha, oven

Dahi, yogurt
Dal, legumes or pulses (lentils, dried peas and beans)
Dalchini, cinnamon
Dhaniya, coriander
Dosa, rice pancakes
Dudh, milk

Elaichi, cardamom

Gajar, carrots
Gatta, chickpea flour balls
Gehun, whole wheat
Ghee, clarified butter
Gobi, cauliflower
Gulab Jal, rose water
Gur, jaggery or raw sugar

Haldi, turmeric
Hari Mirch, green chili
Heeng, asafetida

Imli, tamarind

Jaiphal, nutmeg
Javitri, mace

Kabab Cheeni, allspice
Kaddu, pumpkin
Kaiser, saffron
Kaju, cashew nuts
Kakari, cucumber
Kala Namak, black salt
Kali Mirch, black pepper
Kari Patta, curry leaves
Katori, small bowl
Kela, banana
Khaskhas, poppy seeds
Kismis, raisins
Koela, charcoal

Lahsun, garlic
Lal Mirch, red chili
Lal Moolee, radish
Lauki, green squash
Laung, cloves

Maida, all purpose flour
Maithi, fenugreek
Makhan, butter
Malai, cream
Mangrail, onion seeds
Matar, green peas
Masala, spices
Mirchi, chili
Muli, horseradish
Mungphalli, peanut

Namak, salt
Narangi, oranges

Nariyal, coconut
Naspaati, pears
Neebu, lemon, lime

Paan, betel leaf
Paalak, spinach
Paani, water
Paneer, Indian Cheese
Papita, papaya
Pooha, rice flakes
Pista, pistachios
Podina, mint
Puri, fried whole wheat bread
Pyaaz, onions

Rai, mustard seeds
Roti, bread

Sabzi, vegetable
Sajawat, garnish
Sonf, anise seed
Seb, apple
Sevian, vermicelli
Shalgam, turnip
Shehd, honey
Simla Mirach, bell pepper
Sirka, vinegar
Suji, semolina, Cream of Wheat
Supari, betel nuts

Tamatar, tomato
Tarbuz, watermelon
Tej Patta, bay leaf
Tel, oil
Til, sesame seed

Urad Dal, white split gram beans

Varak, silver foil

Zeera, cumin

index

214

219

NOTES